D1612440

About Island Press

Since 1984, the nonprofit organization Island Press has been stimulating, shaping, and communicating ideas that are essential for solving environmental problems worldwide. With more than 1,000 titles in print and some 30 new releases each year, we are the nation's leading publisher on environmental issues. We identify innovative thinkers and emerging trends in the environmental field. We work with world-renowned experts and authors to develop cross-disciplinary solutions to environmental challenges.

Island Press designs and executes educational campaigns, in conjunction with our authors, to communicate their critical messages in print, in person, and online using the latest technologies, innovative programs, and the media. Our goal is to reach targeted audiences—scientists, policy makers, environmental advocates, urban planners, the media, and concerned citizens—with information that can be used to create the framework for long-term ecological health and human well-being.

Island Press gratefully acknowledges major support from The Bobolink Foundation, Caldera Foundation, The Curtis and Edith Munson Foundation, The Forrest C. and Frances H. Lattner Foundation, The JPB Foundation, The Kresge Foundation, The Summit Charitable Foundation, Inc., and many other generous organizations and individuals.

The opinions expressed in this book are those of the author(s) and do not necessarily reflect the views of our supporters.

Place and Prosperity

Place and Prosperity

HOW CITIES HELP US TO CONNECT AND INNOVATE

William Fulton

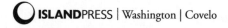
ISLANDPRESS | Washington | Covelo

Library of Congress Control Number: 2021950874

All Island Press books are printed on environmentally responsible materials.

Manufactured in the United States of America
10 9 8 7 6 5 4 3 2 1

Keywords: Auburn, New York; car dependency; downtown; economic renewal; Garden City; gentrification; Houston, Texas; local government; Los Angeles; Main Street; New Urbanism; real estate development; smart growth; suburban sprawl; transportation; urban renewal; Ventura, California; walkability

For Robert H. Fulton Jr. (1915–1985),
who could always find the downtown and the ballpark
in any city almost immediately.

Contents

Foreword

BY RICK COLE

Ages ago, Saint Augustine juxtaposed the City of God and the City of Man. For the past forty years, Bill Fulton has been striving to reconcile the two.

The heavenly city exists only as an ideal. The patron saint of contemporary urbanism, Jane Jacobs, described the earthly city as "organized complexity." Real cities are vibrant, gritty, and dynamic. In a series of widely influential books and articles, Fulton has evaluated city planning theories by analyzing how they actually work in practice. This new collection of essays and case studies lays bare the convergence of place and prosperity—and the divergence between popular nostrums of economic development and the way real people inhabit real places.

As we now understand, starting in the middle of the twentieth century, America's most powerful city makers tried to impose a rigid overlay on cities all across the United States. Their formula was diagrammatic, sterile, and static. They nearly killed cities with their barbaric "urban renewal." Their plans and policies relegated racial minorities to increasingly impoverished ghettoes and replaced human scale with automobile domination. Their misguided schemes coincided with a tectonic shift of capital investment to the suburbs and the hollowing out of America's industrial base.

Fulton stepped into this bleak landscape with the fresh lens of a young journalist raised in an old-school industrial town. He spent the next four decades analyzing what went wrong in our cities and reporting on the increasingly robust stirrings of an authentic urban renaissance. This book is both Fulton's *Bildungsroman*—tracing the arc of his intellectual development—and the chronicle of the great urban comeback of America's cities.

Starting as a "fiercely independent cub reporter," Fulton is the only urban thinker of our time who combines the sharp eye of a journalist, the objective rigor of an academic, and the practical experience of a leader. As he notes, his writing has always been anchored by the complementary poles of place and prosperity.

It is possible for poor places to have beauty and prosperous places to be ugly, but as Fulton repeatedly observes, enduring prosperity is rooted in *attractive* places. Businesses—no matter how successful—and industries—no matter how dominant—rise and fall. As Herbert Stein's Law of Economics bluntly puts it: "Things that can't go on forever, don't." If cities are to be sustained beyond the life cycle of their current economic drivers, they cannot neglect a strategic focus on the always emerging future. As he notes in his introduction, "The most relevant economic development question is not 'What business are you attracting?' but rather 'What do you have left the day after the business leaves?'"

That's taking the long view and the high road. It reflects the foundations of Fulton's worldview, which might best be described as "visionary pragmatism." The essence of "Fultonism" emerged not only from his reporting and academic work, but also from his long years in public service. He served as a planning commissioner for the newly incorporated City of West Hollywood when the municipality was finding its economic footing as a creative center of film, music, entertainment, and design in greater Los Angeles. When he relocated to Ventura on the coast north of Los Angeles, he chaired the citizen panel that produced the Ventura Vision, a strategic guide for the city to move beyond a declining oil-based economy. He was persuaded to run—successfully—for the city council and then went on to serve as mayor. Later, he would be tapped as San Diego's planning director. These leadership responsibilities taught him the stark limitations of armchair critics and their textbook theories.

"No es lo mismo hablar de toros que estar en el redondel," goes the Mexican folk wisdom: talking about the bulls is not the same as being in the arena. Fulton's time in the arena of public service sharpened his insights into how cities actually work.

As mayor of Ventura, he saw firsthand how "free parking" distorted the laws of supply and demand in the city's historic downtown. He had embraced the policy recommendations of his former professor at UCLA, Donald Shoup, who wrote the unlikely best seller *The High Cost of Free Parking.* Patiently, Mayor Fulton explained to downtown merchants and customers that installing parking meters on Main Street would eliminate the perceived parking shortage by shifting cost-conscious customers to the empty parking lots behind the storefronts. But academic theories failed to dissuade dissident local merchants and customers from pursuing a divisive recall effort to oust Fulton from office. Ultimately, the parking meters worked exactly as Fulton predicted, and the recall fizzled—not, however, without marking his mayorship with the "dust and sweat and blood" of *realpolitik.* (You can read about Ventura's downtown ten years later in Chapter 9, "My Favorite Street," where Fulton notes: "Main Street Moves is a whopping success, and it shows what makes a truly great street: It's flexible. It's able to bend to the demands of the moment, rather than rigidly serving one purpose at all times.")

During his time as mayor, Fulton faced similar blowback for his support for a visionary plan to remake an eight-lane suburban arterial running through the center of the newer sections of Ventura. Victoria Avenue is a typical hodgepodge of shopping centers, office buildings, fast-food drive-throughs, and strip malls that could be Anywhere USA. New Urbanist architects and planners sketched out a brilliant long-term evolution. The plan they developed was adopted by the city council, but was quickly overshadowed by a war over reducing traffic lanes on Victoria Avenue and whether to allow a new Walmart to occupy a vacant Kmart (there wasn't much choice). The hoped-for transformation has yet to take place.

These humbling experiences reinforced Fulton's congenital skepticism of high-flown concepts that aren't rooted in reality. Yet one of his most significant economic development breakthroughs came from his willingness to take a risk most elected officials would recoil from even suggesting.

Fulton's decades of exposure to flavor-of-the-month "big bang" panaceas to save cities (build a stadium, a convention center, a festival marketplace, a blockbuster museum!) conversely taught him the value of thinking small. With some colleagues, Fulton persuaded the majority of the council to turn a vacant office building behind City Hall into incubator space for local entrepreneurs and to invest $5 million of city reserves in a private venture capital fund that pledged to invest in local start-ups outside Silicon Valley, including in Ventura. The city ultimately profited from the fund and successfully launched The Trade Desk, which runs a trading platform that allows customers to purchase various types of ads to run global campaigns in digital media. From its start as a single desk in the city-sponsored incubator, The Trade Desk moved to its own large downtown office space, where it has become one of the most successful "ad tech" companies in the world. Such experiences honed Fulton the skeptical critic, Fulton the thoughtful professor, and Fulton the visionary leader into Fulton the rigorous analyst of urban economics and placemaking.

The stories gathered here cover the decades from the urban crisis of the 1960s to the unfolding challenges of today. They illuminate the dramatic transformation of US cities, big and small. Fulton traces the evolution of Auburn, New York, the factory town where he grew up. In other essays, he relates the desperate efforts of struggling communities to persuade corporations to remain—and the even more pathetic pursuit of "'romancing the smokestack'—wooing some out-of-town business in hopes that it will come to town." His stories are rich and varied, full of colorful characters and commentary.

In many of these stories, Fulton zeroes in on the parade of panaceas that have afflicted cities hoping for postindustrial deliverance. His keen insights debunk fevered hype and false hope. Whether it's sports, culture, tech, or tourism, he keeps reminding us that "there is no magic bullet for prosperity." The intoxicating ribbon cuttings inevitably lead to sobering reality checks.

Nor does Fulton spare the "next big thing" in theories of urban development. Richard Florida's *The Rise of the Creative Class* imbued cynical hucksters and gullible politicians with the crackbrain idea that grunge bands and gay bars could point the way to reviving Rust Belt towns. In Chapter 13, "Kotkin versus Florida," Fulton explores not a landmark Supreme Court case, but the nuanced debate between the "creative class" notions of Florida and the concept of "nerdistans" championed by contrarian author Joel Kotkin. He gives both arguments their due while deploring the either-or tone of their dispute.

Repeatedly, Fulton detects the flaws in black-and-white Manichean perspectives and continually looks for the "both-and" synthesis. That may explain why, despite his reputation for authoritative perspectives, he has never emerged as a hot headliner for the big annual conventions where architects, planners, developers, local elected officials, or economic development professionals gather. In our attention deficit democracy, Fulton refuses to reduce his ideas to a slick TED Talk—or 140 characters.

That reticence, however, is precisely the reason to pay attention to Fulton's work. When he asserts that "at its core, prosperity is not about a single business, but about the permanent assets that an economic development effort creates," he's conveying a timeless truth. His varied stories convey the challenges, nuances, and paradoxes of what it takes to make and maintain places that people love—places that hold their value over time. As Jacobs wrote in her classic, *The Death and Life of Great American Cities*: "We may wish for easier, all-purpose analyses and simpler, magical, all-purpose cures, but wishing cannot change these problems into simpler matters than organized complexity, no matter how we try to evade the realities." The stories Fulton recounts in this book uncover how timeless principles play out in real time and in real places and discern how diverse cities adapt and improve or stagnate and decline.

Ultimately, it is the application of that understanding to our challenges today that most commands Fulton's attention—and that he insists should command ours. As he writes in his introduction: "If cities as places and cradles of prosperity are the result of intentional human actions—decisions by people with political or economic power—the revival of cities in the United States during my working life has come about because mayors and other local leaders have learned anew how to use intentional decisions to make those cities better."

Of all those impactful leaders, perhaps the most compelling figure in these pages is the legendary thinker and doer who guided modern-day Philadelphia through its postwar evolution. In Chapter 4, "The Autocratic Citizen of Philadelphia," Fulton recounts the saga of Ed Bacon, who "had an artist's vision and a monarch's will." If New York City's Robert Moses is now contrasted as the malevolent foil to the saintly Jane Jacobs, Fulton paints a more benevolent portrait of Bacon as the power broker of the City of Brotherly Love. As always, however, Fulton gives both sides of the story: "Tethered to such a strong personal vision and a strong personal will, Bacon did not seem to notice or care about the city's changing demographics or the growing significance of race and class in planning discussions, and eventually that made him seem old-fashioned and out of date."

So if Bacon's weak spots teach us that we can't rely on "decisions by people with political or economic power" to overcome today's daunting challenges, what then? In the face of global market meltdowns, pandemics, climate change, and disruptive technology, as well as deepening racial, social, and economic divides, who will produce the "intentional human actions" that can sustain our urban habitats across the United States—and around the world?

If you haven't campaigned for and won office in the retail politics of your hometown city hall as Fulton has, it is impossible to fully appreciate the strengths and shortcomings of local democracy. Fulton knows how poorly informed and preoccupied voters can be, but he's compiled this book for us, the people who inhabit the neighborhoods, communities, and regions that encompass both America's present and future. Fulton insists on puncturing our delusions while also broadening our horizons. He's right when he says that "most of us never think about the idea of place; usually, we just drift from place to place every day without consciously processing the experience. But whether we are in a city, in the suburbs, or out in the countryside, we intuitively understand place—we know whether we like the place we're in or not."

That intuitive understanding of place carries the potential to awaken public citizens from their private cocoons. Fulton the skeptic still maintains a guarded faith in our potential to act as champions of the places we call home—to make intentional economic and political decisions to sustain and improve those places for ourselves and future generations. His stories stand as stark warnings against short-sightedness, and his lessons reinforce our better instincts. Fulton reminds us that we are fallible and capable of folly. Still, he places his hope in the certainty that "better cities emerge when the people who shape them think more broadly and consciously about the places they are creating."

Preface

One evening in December of 1978—at the beginning of a miserably snowy winter that turned out, not surprisingly, to be my last in Upstate New York—my old friend Gary Kromer and I sat around his dorm room at Syracuse University drinking beer and shooting the breeze. I didn't realize at the time what a pivotal moment it was for my life and future career.

Gary was getting a doctorate in mass communications at the Newhouse School—he went on to a long career as research director at the *Fort Worth Star-Telegram*—and he was fascinated by the way newspapers were slicing their readership into smaller pieces they could sell ads to. For example, newspapers were beginning to create "zoned" editions in suburban areas to cater to local advertisers. From Gary's point of view, watching how the business of newspapers was changing, I was exhibit number one because, as one of the first suburban zone reporters ever hired by the *Syracuse Post-Standard*, I was constantly roaming suburbs like Baldwinsville, Liverpool, and North Syracuse for the newspaper's "Neighbors North" section. In today's parlance, I was producing the hyperlocal "content" that the newspaper could sell ads against.

As a ferociously independent cub reporter, I didn't want to see that this job—my first job out of college—was simply to provide the backdrop against which to sell ads. Rather, I viewed myself as engaged in public service—the journalism equivalent of a VISTA volunteer (with a paycheck to match)—doggedly pursuing local stories to help a local leadership be better informed, and the world I had parachuted into was fascinating. It was an endless swirl of town board, village board, planning board, and school board meetings where virtually the only topic of conversation was the physical growth of the community: new subdivisions, new houses, new strip shopping centers, how many new sewer trunk lines would be required to carry away the waste from these projects, how many children these new subdivisions would produce that the schools would have to educate, and, above all else, what the property tax rate would have to be to provide all the necessary services to these burgeoning suburbs.

"This planning stuff is pretty interesting," I said. "I wonder how you become a planner?"

"I dunno," Gary said in response, "I guess maybe you go to, maybe, planning school!"

And then, gulping our beer, we both laughed uproariously at the idea that there might be such a thing as *planning school.*

As it turned out, not only was there such a thing as planning school, but Syracuse University had a respected planning curriculum at the time, and the *Post-Standard* had a policy of paying tuition for employees pursuing higher education. A month later, at age twenty-three, I enrolled in my first-ever graduate-level urban planning course, taught by a crusty but insightful guy named Bob Bartels, who had at one time been planning director of Hartford, Connecticut. At the same time, I returned from exile in the northern suburbs to the downtown newsroom, where as a general-assignment reporter I covered my first truly big urban planning story: The planning and construction of the university's

Carrier Dome, which, as it turned out, was the first test of a new state environmental review law. I was off and running.

Like every other cub reporter in the 1970s, I was energized by the Watergate scandal and *All the President's Men.* As a friend of mine once put it, I was also—like many young reporters—tyrannized by ambition. I didn't really care whom I stepped on or how much I moved around. I just wanted to uncover great stories—preferably ones that put politicians in jail—and move up the ladder to the *New York Times* or the *Washington Post.* So, at the end of the 1970s, I left my reporter job in Syracuse and moved to Washington, DC, to attend graduate journalism school at American University, hoping to jump-start my move up the ladder.

But there was something about cities—in particular, the way cities were climbing out of the hole in the early 1980s—that changed how I thought about everything. The whole concept of experiencing place was baked into me from an early age. In journalism school at American, I drifted away from standard political reporting and began to write about cities and places. (I took all my electives in urban planning at George Washington University; at the time, both universities were part of a reciprocal consortium.) After I finished my degree, I moved as far away as I could—to this day I am still not quite sure why—and began what turned out to be a decades-long effort to understand that most unusual and yet most American of all cities: Los Angeles.

I went back to graduate school one more time, this time for urban planning at the UCLA, but my goal was still not to be a planner. Rather, I wanted to establish my credentials as an authoritative writer about cities and urban planning. Along the way, while still in planning school full-time, I got a push: The suburban editor of the *Los Angeles Times* declined to hire me as a reporter. I was devastated at the time, but it was the greatest gift anybody ever gave me because it freed me of being tyrannized by ambition as a journalist. I began to make the transition to planner.

This transition was, at first, almost imperceptible. But I was extraordinarily lucky to be starting out in Los Angeles when I did. Although traditionally dismissed by East Coast urbanists, Los Angeles in the 1980s was coming into its own as a world city. And I got some amazing breaks almost immediately. Within a month of arriving, I had found work as a temp at a consulting firm specializing in redevelopment financing (a topic that would engage me for decades, especially as mayor thirty years later) and gotten an internship at the regional planning agency, the Southern California Association of Governments. A few months after arriving, I was present at the victory party for the rent control movement in Santa Monica, a seminal event, as it turned out, in Southern California development politics. Soon I was spending a lot of time at UCLA's libraries researching the development history of Los Angeles. Without quite realizing it, I had found my subject—although it took sixteen more years for me to conceive of, write, and publish *The Reluctant Metropolis: The Politics of Urban Growth in Los Angeles*.

After graduate school in planning at UCLA, I set up shop as a freelance writer on urban planning issues. This seemed like a laughable concept to most people at the time, but somehow I made it work. I wrote about anything and everything about Los Angeles for anybody who would pay me: a business magazine, a magazine for lawyers, *Planning* magazine (published by the American Planning Association), the *Los Angeles Times* real estate section (which was surprisingly lively in those days, in between the ads for fancy homes), a London-based publication that covered real estate markets worldwide. Eventually, I landed on a few lasting clients, including *Governing* magazine (for which I wrote for more than thirty years, until the magazine's print edition finally folded) and the Sunday Opinion section of the *Los Angeles Times*.

And in 1984 I got what was, in retrospect, another fabulously lucky break. I was living in West Hollywood—WeHo, for short—at the time an unincorporated community squeezed between Hollywood and

Beverly Hills. WeHo was the center of gay life in Los Angeles, but it was also the epicenter of a real estate boom that was driving up rents—and fast. Fearful that Los Angeles County would eliminate rent control, WeHo activists quickly began a move toward—and successful vote for—incorporation as a city, a movement I participated in. Although incorporation was driven by concerns about rent control, WeHo got national publicity in 1984 when voters elected the first majority gay city council in US history.

After the city was incorporated, I became active in discussions about its future growth. As a result, barely thirty years old, a year out of planning school and still a struggling journalist—at a time when my classmates were still interns at various small cities around Los Angeles—I wound up as chair of the planning commission in one of the hottest cities in the United States. Suddenly I was immersed in the minutia of urban planning—parking regulations and zoning requirements—while simultaneously dealing with some of the most famous people in the world. For example, during my tenure, architect César Pelli's expansion of the Pacific Design Center was built, but producer David Geffen's proposed new building on the Sunset Strip was not.

For a kid from a declining factory town in Upstate New York, it was a pretty heady experience. In retrospect, however, it was an early experience with urban revitalization and gentrification. Like so many other city neighborhoods, WeHo had been hip but sketchy in the 1970s but now was attracting high-end investment. Like the rest of the Westside of Los Angeles, WeHo eventually went so far upscale that there's no way I could afford to live there today.

Meanwhile, the real estate boom of the 1980s was on, and California's first serious "slow growth" movement was blooming. All across the state, activists were using lawsuits and ballot measures to kill, stop, slow down, and drag out real estate development projects they didn't like. I was fascinated with this movement because I truly began to see that *places*—the spatial arrangement of people and the locations that they use on a daily basis—were the result of deliberate and (in California at least) mostly political decisions made week after week at planning commission and city council meetings. I also began to see—with the help of people I met along the way, like Henry Cisneros, then mayor of San Antonio, Texas—that cities were the engines of *prosperity*. The very density and proximity to activities that made cities so exciting to live in also made them ideal for hatching businesses and exchanging goods, often bringing economic well-being to everyone in the vicinity.

I began to write about these trends in detail, especially in a publication I started myself, *California Planning & Development*. For personal reasons, my wife and I moved to Ventura, sixty miles up the coast from Los Angeles. One day, a quirky older guy with flowing white hair named Warren Jones showed up and asked to meet with me. He owned a small publishing company that specialized in California planning and environmental law, and he asked me to write a primer on planning in California.

Warren and I had imagined the book to be a desk reference for planners and maybe an introductory primer for newly appointed planning commissioners, but *Guide to California Planning* quickly became the standard textbook on urban planning read by all planning students in California. Almost literally, I went to sleep one night as a journalist writing about real estate, and I woke up the next morning as a guru of urban planning in California.

So, after more than forty years and much to my surprise, here we are. I am not a journalist anymore. I'm a trained and experienced urban planner who has devoted my entire life to making cities better. I've been an urban planning professor, a mayor, the planning director of a big city, a partner in an urban planning firm, the policy director of a nonprofit organization advocating for better development patterns, and the director of an urban think tank in one of America's great cities. Although I grew up in the Snowbelt of Upstate New York—an experience that shaped me more than I can say, as the first essay in this book explains—I have spent most of my career in the Sun Belt, a section of the country I gave nary a thought to while growing up.

As I put this collection together, I am surprised at how often I return in my journey as an urbanist to my two hometowns—Auburn, New York, where I was born and raised, and Ventura, California, where I lived most of my adult life. As the first piece in this collection points out, these two places have shaped me both as an urbanist and as a person more than I can say. Neither is a big city, but they both have long histories as regional centers of commerce and government dating to the nineteenth century. Both were industrial centers—manufacturing in Auburn's case, oil in Ventura's—yet also served as a focal point for agriculture from the surrounding region. Well into the 1960s, both cities had a downtown that served as the focal point for retail and office activity for their county. Both downtowns have been reinvented as centers of arts, entertainment, and food. And both cities still maintain a rare characteristic for American communities today: They still operate, at least somewhat, as somewhat self-contained small urban gems where you see the same people at work, at school, at soccer practice, and in the grocery store.

I keep thinking what a miracle it is—after all the urban decay, urban renewal, freeway construction, and failed efforts at revitalization we have seen in cities in the United States during my lifetime—that these two smallish and somewhat out-of-the-way places, like so many other small cities, have managed to weather the storm and come out with their sense of dignity and their unique identity intact. I am forever grateful to the people of these two cities for helping me understand how valuable urbanism is to our everyday life and how durable that idea truly is.

Introduction

Throughout my career as an urban planning professor, a mayor, the planning director of a big city, a partner in an urban planning firm, the policy director of a nonprofit organization advocating for better development patterns, and the director of an urban think tank, I've never stopped writing about cities—most especially about how cities are rooted in place, how cities are engines of prosperity, and how these two things are deeply intertwined.

Although the essays in this book are in some ways personal, drawing on my own experience in learning and writing about cities, their primary purpose is to show how these two ideas—*place* and *prosperity*—lie at the heart of what a city is and, by extension, what our society is all about. Although these essays were written over a period of time, I have updated many of them to reflect current conditions.

Of all the concepts discussed in this book, none is more fundamental than the idea of *place*. Cities are first of all places—specific locations that serve as centers of human activity.

At its core, place is a pretty simple concept: It's a particular geographical location. And place is one of the most common and ubiquitous of all human experiences. We are *always* situated in a particular location—our home, our car, our workplace, the places we typically shop, our church or other place of worship—and most often they are the *same* locations from one day to the next. As we travel, our physical environment is constantly changing. We are indoors, we are outdoors, or we are somewhere in between. We travel on foot, on a bus or train, in a car or truck. The world gets warmer or cooler, lighter or darker. We are surrounded by tall buildings or parking lots or open fields or some combination of all three.

Most of us never think about the idea of place; usually, we just drift from place to place every day without consciously processing the experience. But whether we are in a city, in the suburbs, or out in the countryside, we intuitively understand place—we know whether we like the place we're in or not.

And we all feel an intense emotional connection to places that are important to us and to other people who feel that same connection. There are few more powerful questions than, "Where are you from" or "Where do you live?" That's why people fight so hard to retain qualities of place they value, whether that's protecting the single-family neighborhood where they raised their kids or a piece of nature they like to visit.

What is not always obvious is that the places we experience—the places we like or dislike—are the result of deliberate decisions made by all kinds of people. Most of these decisions are small ones made by individuals: the flowers you plant in your garden, the color you paint your house, where you park your car. But if you zoom out to look at the entire landscape—urban or natural—you begin to understand that those landscapes were created in large part through big, important decisions made by people with political or economic power.

Rural landscapes throughout the United States, for example, were created by farmers for economic reasons. As result, there are few forests left in Upstate New York and few prairies left in the Midwest. Where natural landscapes remain, mostly in the West, it is largely the result of political decisions by state and federal governmental agencies. Similarly, urban landscapes have been created over a period of centuries by individual families, merchants, industrialists, and—thanks to urban renewal and other such programs—government agencies. And over the past century, suburban landscapes have been created out of whole cloth by real estate developers and their urban planners and engineers.

So, to understand place—and understand human settlements generally—it is important to understand that places are not created by accident. They are created on purpose to further a political or economic agenda. Better cities emerge when the people who shape them think more broadly and consciously about the places they are creating. Many of the essays in this book describe the process by which these decisions are made.

As fundamental as the concept of place is to the ideas in this book, place cannot really be separated from prosperity. For thousands of years, cities have existed in large part as vehicles of commerce—locations where people come together, knowledge and goods are exchanged, raw materials are transformed into manufactured goods, and, in some cases, goods are simply transferred from one form of transportation to another (a process known in the goods movement business as transshipment). As much as we urban planners like to think of cities primarily as places to live—and our jobs as creating great places to live on a day-to-day basis—cities live or die, and people live fulfilling lives or not primarily because of those cities succeed or fail as engines of prosperity.

If cities as places and cradles of prosperity are the result of intentional human actions—decisions by people with political or economic power—the revival of cities in the United States during my working life has come about because mayors and other local leaders have learned anew how to use intentional decisions to make those cities better.

Like so many other things in American life, cities hit bottom during the 1970s, when I was just starting out. Virtually all urban neighborhoods were depopulating in those days—not just in Detroit, but also in Los Angeles, San Francisco, Seattle, and many other cities that today we think of as thriving. Now-gentrified places such as Oakland and Brooklyn were, at the time, national symbols of racial strife and the underlying unrest in American society. The greatest city of them all—New York—lost a million people and went bankrupt in that decade.

Out of these depths emerged an urban renaissance led, initially, by strong and innovative mayors like Henry Cisneros in San Antonio, Bill Hudnut in Indianapolis, Charles Royer in Seattle, even Richard M. Daley in Chicago. At first, there was a tendency among these politicians to focus on big, splashy projects—things like convention centers, sports stadiums, and auto assembly plants that would make headlines and perhaps, on their own, change the trajectory of a declining city.

Over time, however, these mayors and other civic leaders learned many lessons about how to do economic development right: how to nurture entrepreneurs and young businesses, how to build the ecosystems that businesses need to survive, how to attract talent. In a way, there was nothing new about this. Throughout history, cities have emerged in particular locations for the reasons described above. But over time they often prosper—or not—based on their ability to adapt to new conditions and move beyond their original purpose.

Think of Boston, for example. How is it that, over a period of hundreds of years, a place that was basically a seafaring town turned into the world's leading center for higher education? How did Pittsburgh, a steel town, successfully reinvent itself in large part by leveraging the assets of one fairly small university, Carnegie Mellon? Why has Pittsburgh thrived while the Great Lakes cities—Detroit, Cleveland, Buffalo—have struggled so much to adapt to postindustrial conditions? Perhaps most miraculous of all, how did Silicon Valley, which in the 1950s and

'60s was primarily a manufacturing center for electronics, transform itself into the high-tech center of the world? How will cities deal with the fallout from the COVID-19 pandemic?

The answers lie in the relationship between place and prosperity and the vision that each city's leaders bring to the task of using place as a platform for prosperity. A city's prosperity over time does not depend on one individual business, no matter how large it might be or how splashy an announcement the mayor made when that business arrived in town. Rather, prosperity depends on using businesses to build assets in a particular place that can be recycled. Those assets might be a labor force, a university, a port or airport, or the wealth created by previous generations. That's why Silicon Valley and Pittsburgh are successful: they have recycled wealth and knowledge through their local universities to create a new generation of prosperity. That's why Boston has succeeded in being a dozen different cities over four hundred years. That's why my hometown of Auburn, New York, is still a successful manufacturing town—because after two hundred years, people still know how to make stuff and they love doing it. Over time, a successful place creates enduring economic assets that don't go away and lays the groundwork for prosperity in the future.

At its core, prosperity is not about a single business, but about the permanent assets that an economic development effort creates. The most relevant economic development question is not "What business are you attracting?" but rather "What do you have left the day after the business leaves?"

The answer, to come full circle, is *place*—the character and the quality of the location that you're selling to businesses in the first place. In the industrial era, this usually meant proximity to natural resources or transportation routes. Today, it more often means providing both urban and natural amenities attractive to the smart folks who drive the innovation economy. In my adopted hometown of Ventura, California, the city's most successful company was the outdoor clothing company Patagonia, which was located on the outskirts of downtown for one simple reason: The founder, Yvon Chouinard, liked surfing there. To this day, one of the selling points about working at Patagonia is surfing at lunchtime.

Today, cities are no longer at the bottom, as they were when I started writing about them in the 1970s. Rather, many of them are at the top, perhaps so high that they are beginning to topple over. Affluent residents in cities are clearly engaged in what sociologists have come to call "opportunity hoarding"—gathering urban amenities around them in a way that excludes others. And too many are being left behind.

But cities are resilient. They've been buffeted over the decades by White flight, decay, urban renewal, unequal investment, increasingly extreme weather events, and now the worst pandemic in a century, and they're still going strong. At their best, they not only inspire and uplift us, but they make our daily life more convenient, more fulfilling, and more prosperous.

PART 1

PLACE

I used to think that there was such a thing as a "place gene" that some people have and some people don't. How else do you explain how sensitive some people are to every aspect of the urban environment while others are not? But the more I have thought about it—and the more I have worked on the essays in this section—the more I have realized what an arrogant point of view that is. As I noted in the introduction, everybody experiences place. It is part of every single person's everyday life. To paraphrase Winston Churchill, we shape our places and then they shape us.

The essays in this part of the book span a range of places (and a range of times), ranging from Houston to San Diego to Los Angeles to Philadelphia to planned new towns such as Mariemont, Ohio, and Greenbelt, Maryland. But as I prepared these essays for publication, I was struck by two things.

The first is how often I return to my own hometowns, the small cities of Auburn, New York, and Ventura, California. It's remarkable how these two places—not New York City or Los Angeles or London—have shaped my view of cities and how they work.

The second thing that struck me is how much these essays have to do not just with place but with how you get around from one place to another. Walking, driving, taking the bus, navigating an often overwhelming transportation infrastructure—these are consistent themes in my writing about place, just as they are consistent themes in anybody's daily life in a city. Too often we think of transportation as a completely separate topic from place, and we do that to our detriment. No matter whether we are talking about Houston or Auburn, it's important to remember that getting from one place to another is a critical component of understanding and experiencing place.

CHAPTER 1

The Making of an Urbanist

One warm summer's day in 1974, when I was a college kid interning as a cub reporter at what was then the Auburn *Citizen-Advertiser*, I left the newspaper's new building on Dill Street in downtown Auburn, New York, and walked three blocks to Memorial City Hall on South Street to cover a meeting of the Auburn City Council—or, to be technically accurate, the Auburn Urban Renewal Agency (AURA), an offshoot of the council. It was like traversing a war zone.

As I walked down Dill Street to North Street, on my left a new arterial road—the Auburn Arterial—was being plowed through the middle of long-established neighborhoods I had known my whole life. Ahead of me, along Market Street, buildings dating to the nineteenth century were being demolished with federal urban renewal funds, making way for the new Loop Road around downtown and opening up access to the Owasco River (which in those days we called the Outlet) for the first time in a century. And as I crossed Genesee Street where North and South Streets met—downtown Auburn's "100 percent corner"—the main street was torn up as the city began a sixteen-year effort to separate the sanitary sewer and the storm sewer. Although I was only eighteen at the time, the city I had known all my life—the *only* city I had ever known in my life—was disappearing before my very eyes.

When I got to the city hall and the city council entered the council chambers from an anteroom, I was in awe—especially of Auburn's legendary mayor, Paul Lattimore. My parents knew everybody in town, including the mayor. Nevertheless, it was the first time I had ever covered the city council, and it was a heady experience. Even at that young age, I somehow had an understanding of how power in a city worked, and I knew I was in the presence of it. At a time when Auburn's factories were closing or moving south—just as they were all across the northern industrial belt—Lattimore had recently gained national publicity by persuading two Japanese companies to open a new steel mill in town. It was clear that all the city-changing activity I had witnessed on my stroll over to city hall had resulted from decisions made in this room.

I was sitting at the press table, which was located not in front of the dais but to the side, so I could see Lattimore behind the dais. After he sat down, he hiked his pants up to the knees, revealing his legs to me (but, because of the dais, to no one else)—which I later realized was his habit during council meetings. The group met briefly as the Auburn City Council and then reconvened as the board of AURA to discuss the notorious Parcel 21.

Parcel 21 was a large, now-vacant property at the corner of Genesee and Osborne Streets almost directly across the street from the city hall. Only a few years before, part of it had housed the Palace Theater, a movie theater dating back to World War I. For much of Auburn's history, most of the parcel had been home to the city's most important factory, the Osborne Works, which, starting around the time of the Civil War, manufactured agricultural combines. The Osborne Works had long ago been sold to International Harvester and moved out of town, and five years earlier some of the old buildings had burned down. Subsequently, the urban renewal agency had condemned all the properties, assembled a large lot, and torn the remaining buildings down. (Fires were a constant problem in Auburn, and urban renewal was in part an effort to get ahead of the arson curve.)

As I sat at the press table looking at Lattimore's bare legs and watching the city council operate, I realized two things. First, in those days before open meetings laws, most of the topics on the agenda had already been discussed in detail behind closed doors in the anteroom. Second—even more alarming—it was clear that, to the council's surprise, the city couldn't find a developer interested in Parcel 21, even though the council members clearly viewed it as the most attractive downtown site that urban renewal had created.

Eventually, after several visits to the corporate headquarters in Rochester, the city persuaded Wegmans, a regional grocery chain, to relocate its Auburn store from a suburban shopping center on the outskirts of the city to Parcel 21. The market was nobody's idea of great urban design—it faced a giant parking lot and presented a blank wall to Genesee Street—but it was better than nothing. Today, almost a half-century later, Wegmans is viewed as the heart and soul of downtown.

Because it was the first city council meeting I had ever attended—and because it dealt with the first urban development challenge I had ever learned about—that meeting from the summer of 1974 is seared in my memory. I didn't know it at the time, but it was the first time I experienced the intersection between the two professions that would define my life: journalism and urban planning. And it would be many, many years before I understood how Auburn and its history—and especially the urban renewal scars that the city experienced in the 1970s—shaped my understanding of cities and, indeed, my entire career.

⌣

It is hard for anyone who has grown up in the United States recently to understand just how self-contained—how totally complete—cities like Auburn were—not just in the nineteenth century or during World Wars I and II, but as recently as the 1960s and 1970s. In my memory, Auburn—a city of barely more than thirty thousand people then—had four local banks, three local jewelers, two local meat markets, and two mainstream local department stores, as well as a locally owned high-end boutique department store, two movie theaters, two or three hotels, a locally owned newspaper and radio station, several locally owned car dealerships, at least three locally owned jewelers, a sporting equipment store, a music store, an iconic diner, a YMCA, a museum that had once been the home of William Seward (Lincoln's secretary of state), a handsome building housing the police and fire departments designed by a distinguished Boston architectural firm, an iconic post office that looked like a castle, innumerable restaurants and bars, a high school, and, believe it not, a maximum-security state prison that had been built by the inmates in 1820. Remarkably enough, all these businesses and institutions were concentrated in a downtown barely six blocks long and three blocks wide.

The downtown was also home to the city hall and the county courthouse, as well as a lively cadre of lawyers and political operatives that revolved around these buildings. Several churches and other civic institutions such as the local library and a historic cemetery were situated on the edge of the downtown, all within easy walking distance. I don't recall going ever to a doctor's office that was not downtown. My family lived in a handsome 1920s doctor/lawyer/merchant neighborhood one mile away.

Elsewhere in the city—which was only two miles long and three miles wide—ethnic neighborhoods clustered around factories, each neighborhood featuring its own shopping district, bars and restaurants, and social clubs. Even into the 1970s these ethnic neighborhoods held firm, with their local groceries and candy stores and churches, almost all of which were Roman Catholic. Auburn also had a popular minor league baseball team (which was the only community-owned, nonprofit team in the United States), as well as thriving recreational softball leagues in the summer and bowling leagues in the winter. The entire city was easily walkable, bikeable, and busable.

My family's life revolved around this small city and especially around the downtown, where everything we might need was located. There were very few reasons you would ever leave town—or look beyond it for anything that had to do with your day-to-day life. You might go to Syracuse or Rochester for a concert or occasionally go to a shopping mall in suburban Syracuse, twenty-five miles away, to get something at a particular store not located in Auburn. Once in a while I couldn't find—or wait for—a book I wanted at our local bookstore and took the bus to Syracuse to get it.

The Fultons had lived in Auburn for more than a hundred years, gradually moving upward from the working class to the middle class. My great-great-grandfather Hugh Fulton, who arrived with his wife and two children from Scotland in 1869, worked in the local textile mills. *His* son, my great-grandfather, also named Hugh, was also trained in textiles and with his brother ran the textile shop at what is now Auburn Correctional Facility, a maximum-security state prison best known as the place where the first execution by electrocution in history took place. *His* son, my grandfather Bob, was apprenticed as a jeweler and eventually ran an electrical supply store—a good business in the early twentieth century, when society was becoming electrified for the first time. And *his* son, my father, also named Bob, went to college and spent a lifetime as a salesman and public relations guy. For more than a hundred years, none of them ever ventured more than two miles away from where they were born for either home or work.

My parents seemed to know everybody. My father had been a rogue school board candidate, and my mother was one of the first women on the city parks and recreation commission, where she focused—to everyone's astonishment—on parks and the civic band rather than on recreational softball, which was viewed by most people as the commission's most important mission. It wasn't surprising that they knew everyone: few families moved in or out. The population had stopped growing when immigration shut down in the 1920s, and everybody had pretty much stayed put ever since.

For all these reasons, life beyond Auburn didn't really exist—or so that's how it seemed to me when I was growing up. We'd have dinner on special occasions in the nearby charming villages of Skaneateles and Aurora. We would occasionally visit relatives in other small Upstate towns, and once a year we'd go on vacation to the Adirondacks. But other than that, we never traveled anywhere. (Indeed, we seemed glued to Upstate New York. One year when our favorite Adirondack resort was closed, we spent our vacation traveling to see other sights, but they were all in Upstate: the St. Lawrence Seaway, Cooperstown, Niagara Falls. We never even went to Pennsylvania.)

Obviously there was a big world out there: I saw it on television and read about it in the three New York newspapers my father bought every day. And as a manufacturing town, Auburn was connected to the world in ways I didn't understand—raw materials flowed in from everywhere, and finished products flowed out to everywhere. But the outside world didn't seem real—or, perhaps more accurately, accessible—to me. My favorite athlete was the enthusiastic and graceful Willie Mays, and I spent many afternoons watching him on television chase fly balls up against the chain-link center-field fence of Candlestick Park. But the idea that San Francisco was an actual place in the real world—a place that I could go to, visit, and experience—was simply something that never occurred to me, even as a teenager.

⌣

Auburn was my entire world, and I was endlessly fascinated by both its built and its natural environment. From the time my parents bought me a two-wheeler for my seventh birthday, I was all over town, looking at everything: leftover corner stores in the middle of residential neighborhoods, gullies and culverts that transported water toward the Outlet, the little waterfalls, the handsome Depression-era schools, the fabulous nineteenth-century mill owners' mansions along South Street, the railroad tracks, the churches (there were more than forty of them), the farmland only a few blocks from town, and most of all the Outlet itself and how it intersected with downtown—the two most prominent features in the city, at least to my mind at the time.

The Outlet was the very reason Auburn existed where it did. The steep drops in elevation from Owasco Lake northwest toward the Seneca River and, eventually, Lake Ontario had attracted the first settlers, who operated grist mills. The factories were located along the river because they had originally used water power. At the time, the Outlet was almost completely invisible downtown because so many buildings had been built backing up to it in the nineteenth century, as was typical everywhere in the United States. Yet even then a good portion of the Outlet was still open, with woods on either side, and I remember weaving in and out of natural and built settings as I aimlessly rode my bike. In those days, no street in town—not even the main drag, Genesee Street, which doubled as US Route 20—was so intimating that a seven-year-old on a bicycle was afraid to cross it.

Most of the buildings in town—especially downtown—dated from the late nineteenth and early twentieth centuries. I was fascinated not only with the buildings themselves, but also with how they had been imposed on a natural landscape that was almost impossible to find. Both Hogan's Meat Market and Hunter's Dinerant were perched on platforms above the Outlet. (Hogan's is long gone because of urban renewal, but Hunter's is still there in the location where Auburn was first founded, sporting perhaps the most iconic sign in town.) Although the Outlet was hard to find, it wasn't impossible. If you found your way to the backsides of the old commercial buildings downtown—sometimes by walking around them, sometimes by ducking through a small doorway or driveway—you were in a completely different and fascinating world: Buildings built on stilts, old loading docks, rusty porches. At home in my sandbox, I regularly tried to re-create the town and these buildings.

Later on, in high school, when I began to drive and had friends from all over the city and not just my neighborhood, I got to know the factory-gate neighborhoods that had been settled a half-century before by Poles, Ukrainians, and Italians. The families lived in modest but comfortable homes, and many of the breadwinners still walked to work, almost literally down the street, in the factories. The biggest and most important factory in town was the prison itself, located along the river less than half a mile from downtown. It did not seem odd to me at the time that many of the prison guards themselves lived in two-story homes across the street from the prison and its guard towers (on a street called, not surprisingly, Wall Street), nor that when you had dinner at Balloon's, the wonderful Italian restaurant on Washington Street, you parked against the back wall of the prison across the street.

Many years later, when I was a practicing urban planner, this type of very concentrated urban development came to be known as *smart growth*—"smart" because it was space-efficient, walkable, and inexpensive to provide services to compared to the suburbs. In those days, it was just the way things worked. But "growth" never entered my mind simply because there wasn't any. Auburn's urban patterns as I knew them growing up had been more or less set before World War I; they expanded somewhat in the 1920s, but were stagnant during the Great Depression and World War II. The factories were still mostly thriving in the postwar era, but the population of the city was not growing, and the postwar suburban boom almost completely bypassed Auburn. A few houses were built on the outskirts of town and out on Owasco Lake, but suburban production homebuilding was nonexistent. The 1920s subdivision where I grew up was still being built out in the 1960s—so slowly that I didn't realize I lived in a subdivision at all.

This period of stability coincided with the life span of my parents, both of whom were born around World War I. My father had an amazing ability to absorb and understand Auburn's physical environment and what it meant—an ability he passed on to me, even though I wasn't consciously aware of it at the time.

My dad was a salesman and a public relations guy. There was no reason to think that he had any particular intuition or insight into how cities worked, yet he had an instinctive feel for cities. My mom used to say that they could drive into any town and he immediately find the downtown and the ballpark. (He also loved trains and especially the long-gone interurbans, which connected Auburn to Syracuse and Rochester when he was a kid.) He loved all the things that made Auburn distinctive before urban renewal, especially the businesses downtown like the local soda fountain, where he had gone as a kid and still bought ribbon candy at Christmas. His uncle, Bill Fulton, had operated a jewelry shop on Genesee Street for decades.

My father was the kind of guy who always wanted to be in the middle of what was going on in Auburn. When the Osborne Mill caught fire in 1969—helping create the vacant lot that became Parcel 21—most people in town got in their cars and drove away from it. Our whole family, on the other hand, got in the car and drove toward it. Dad knew that this fire was an important event that would change the city's physical environment, and he wanted to witness it.

From him I learned one of the most important lessons of my life, one that has always caused me to favor cities and villages over suburbs: as wonderful as your home can be, it is not enough all by itself. You have to look beyond your own home to fulfill yourself on a daily basis. Or, as I have often said over the years, my town is my house.

My father also understood how the town worked—how things got done—and he understood the relationship between the power structure and the city itself. He knew the mayor and the general manager of the radio station and the prominent merchants and lawyers, but he also knew the cops and the firefighters and the bus drivers. They had all gone to high school together, and he saw how it all fit together. He understood intuitively what I did not understand until I was a reporter: that all that demolition and change I saw on my walk from the *Citizen-Advertiser* building to the city hall occurred because of the decisions made inside that city hall, which in turn were influenced by a wide variety of interest groups in town, ranging from the chamber of commerce to the police union to the Mafia. So it was not surprising that when the urban renewal reckoning finally came, it broke my father's heart.

In 1965, a central business district subcommittee of the Auburn Planning Board, then led by future mayor Paul Lattimore, released a study of downtown Auburn's conditions. I am in possession of a copy because of an incredible coincidence: thirty-five years later, when I was living in Ventura, California, I was given a copy by Dick Maggio, planning director of nearby Oxnard, who had worked on the document as a young planner in Auburn.

The report itself makes for sobering reading. While acknowledging that the downtown was still the commercial center of Auburn and surrounding Cayuga County, it raised a number of red flags. Downtown's advantage was already being undermined by strip shopping centers nearby. (The only reason a full-fledged regional mall did not exist was that the city hadn't grown in population since the 1920s. The planning board could see that a mall was coming sooner or later—and it did when the notorious Pyramid Company of Syracuse opened Fingerlakes Mall in 1980.) Even so, there were two lingering problems: downtown was extremely congested by traffic—only ten cars at a time could make it through the traffic signal at the main intersection—and the nineteenth-century commercial buildings throughout downtown had long since become obsolete. Something needed to be done.

Thus was born the Auburn Urban Renewal Agency. It wasn't an unusual move at the time: backed by federal funds, urban renewal was a trend throughout the United States. "Obsolete" buildings and districts were razed all over the country in the name of "slum clearance." In Auburn, as in many other cities, the goal was not just to remove so-called slums but to revitalize a struggling downtown business district by making it more competitive with suburban shopping centers. As a result of the 1965 analysis, AURA came up with a huge and daring plan: Tear down half the buildings in the downtown and build a loop road around downtown to facilitate traffic flow and revitalize commerce. The federal government was happy to give Auburn the money to do so, just as it gave the money to hundreds of cities around the United States for similar efforts. And many business owners—already struggling and saddled with nineteenth-century buildings—were just as happy to get paid off to go out of business.

At more or less the same time, the state of New York was working on its own plan to clear out the traffic congestion on US Route 20 (and New York State Route 5) through downtown Auburn. Several routes were considered, including a route that would have completely bypassed the city. But in typical fashion, many Auburn small business owners feared that they would lose too much business if traffic didn't go by their stores and therefore lobbied for a route that went through the center of town, just two blocks to the north of Genesee Street.

As a result, in the early 1970s, at the same time the city was razing half of downtown and building Loop Road, the state was building the

Auburn Arterial just to the north, demolishing two hundred structures and eliminating century-old neighborhoods in the process. Uncharacteristically—but mercifully—the historically Black neighborhood was spared, largely because it was located adjacent to the historic district containing the nineteenth-century mill owners' mansions south of downtown, away from the through highways.

The city's leaders thought that they were saving the town.

But they could not have predicted the current they would be swimming against. The 1970s turned out to be the era when factories began to shutter all over Upstate New York and ambitious young people—like me—left for economic opportunity elsewhere. The result was that AURA had set the table for developers to take advantage of a market that no longer existed. For almost half a century, downtown Auburn has existed in a kind of statis: half a beautiful historic town, half a wasteland, waiting for the market to return.

By the time the devastation was complete, my father had lived in Auburn for more than sixty years—his entire life except for a short time at college in Michigan. The city defined him, consumed him. He was full of stories about the city and its places, especially the downtown, where virtually all the important experiences of his life had occurred. But after urban renewal and the arterial, he and my mother retired to the Adirondacks, and he never looked back.

It took me a long time—almost forty years—to realize that I too was heartbroken about what happened to Auburn and that this heartbreak had actually defined my career, both as a journalist and an urban planner. In recent years I have jokingly referred to my urban PTSD—the trauma I experienced when, as a high school and college kid, I watched my beautiful historic little city be half-demolished. It is perhaps no surprise, then, that I left Auburn behind for a long time and moved to

Aerial view of Auburn, New York, before (top) and after (bottom) urban renewal
(Credit: Bill Hecht)

Southern California—about as far away from Auburn as you can get and still be in the contiguous United States—and I didn't come back much for twenty years.

On that journey, I kept looking for *my* Auburn—a place that some-how combined a small scale with the concentrated urbanism that I knew as a kid. But at the time I was looking, it seemed impossible to imagine that this kind of small-town urbanism would ever exist again anywhere in the United States. At that time, it was hard enough to imagine strong, vibrant cities of any size. Even very large cities like New York and Phil-adelphia were struggling.

When I left Upstate New York for good in 1980, the United States was a solidly suburban country, with cities still strongly in retreat. For no particular reason, I landed in Los Angeles—the epitome of the sub-urban United States. LA was a low-rise, auto-oriented place that had served for more fifty years as a kind of national suburb—a place where people from all over the county could escape places like Auburn that boxed them in and build a prosperous, happy, and auto-oriented life. Although LA was fascinating—so fascinating that I wrote *The Reluc-tant Metropolis* about it—it was also alienating. I was pretty sure that I would never experience anything like the walkable, small-scale urban-ism I knew as a kid.

As it happened, however, the 1980s turned out to be a time when people began to rediscover the experience of cities. This was when gen-trification began—when we first began to see Brooklyn and Oakland and Hoboken gain new residents and new investment. And, surpris-ingly, Los Angeles turned out to be a great place to look for the small-scale urbanism I missed.

The Los Angeles area seems unplanned, but as Greg Hise wrote in *Magnetic Los Angeles*, much of it was deliberately planned: Small-scale downtowns surrounded by working-class neighborhoods close to a nearby factory or plant (including, in some cases, a movie studio—no less of a factory to Los Angeles than the prison was to Auburn). These neighborhoods were connected—in the early twentieth century, at

THE MAKING OF AN URBANIST   23

least—by the most extensive interurban rail system in the United States. Although by the 1980s Los Angeles County was defined primarily by its freeway system, it was dotted with small-scale downtowns on the verge of bouncing back. The most famous are Pasadena and Santa Monica, but there are dozens more, and I intuitively understood this form of urban development.

The beach town of Ventura was not literally one of these old inter-urban suburbs, but it was definitely the same kind of place. Sixty miles from downtown Los Angeles, on the road to Santa Barbara, it was far enough removed from the city that it was not really integrated into the region's larger commuting pattern. But it was historically a working-class place without much pretension, and it was one of the oldest cities in Southern California. By the 1980s, it was largely suburban in a way that Auburn was not because, unlike Auburn, Ventura had not been bypassed by postwar suburban growth. Here the downtown that had once been the center of everything was in transition, and day-to-day retail activity had moved to shopping malls on the edge of town.

The remnants of an Auburn-type urban history remained in down-town Ventura nonetheless—the Knights of Columbus, the Masonic Temple, the Elks Club, the bank on the main corner of downtown, the downtown movie palace that was now a live music venue, the 1920s building where all the lawyers had historically had their offices, a downtown post office, locally owned camera and stationery stores, and a beautiful Beaux-Arts county courthouse that was now the city hall. There was even, just to the west of downtown, a kind of factory-gate neighborhood with modest homes from the 1910s and 1920s for work-ing families—the factory being the nearby oil fields.

Ventura was not without its scars from urban renewal. In the 1960s, California Highway 101 (the "Ventura Highway" from the 1972 hit song) had plowed a path through the center of Ventura between downtown and the beach. Thankfully, the historic downtown was spared, but the beachfront area was redeveloped with an uninspiring collection of condominiums, apartments, and hotels.

The older part of town was still eminently walkable and bikeable, however, and a fair number of people lived there without owning a car. And given what I learned from my father back in Auburn, it was not hard to figure out how the town worked—how the power to get things done radiated from the politicians, the business leaders, the police department, and the rest of the civic infrastructure. Once again, I could see how decisions made by the power structure affected how the city worked and how the whole physical environment of the city was structured—a power structure I eventually became part of as an elected city council member and mayor.

Most astonishingly, as the county seat and historic center of oil and agriculture in Ventura County, Ventura was pretty self-contained— much as Auburn was when I was a kid. Far more than other Southern California towns, it was a place where you could live your whole life. Most people who lived in town worked in town, so the people you saw at work were also the people you saw at the farmers' market or at your kids' soccer practice. In the twenty-five years that I lived there— and, in particular, the eight years that I served on the Ventura City Council—I fought fiercely for the idea that the city should remain a self-contained place and not deteriorate into a mere bedroom suburb or retirement town.

In other words, Auburn shaped my approach to Ventura more than I can say. Twenty-seven hundred miles from home, my town was still my house.

In recent years, I have not lived in Ventura, but I have returned to Auburn more frequently than I used to. Like most of Upstate New York, Auburn still struggles economically. The retail businesses that fled downtown for the mall have had a tough time, as the mall has fought a losing battle against the local Walmart, where the parking lot is perpetually full to overflowing.

Downtown Auburn has seen few new buildings constructed—a turn of events that Paul Lattimore and the civic leaders of the 1960s and 1970s never expected—but after fifty years of urban renewal, downtown still has many gaps. The Wegmans grocery store still presents a blank wall to Genesee Street, the main drag in town. Most Auburnians are accustomed to the Outlet—now commonly referred to as the Owasco River—as an open feature of downtown rather than something hidden behind nineteenth-century buildings.

Still, a lack of building does not mean a lack of investment. Downtown Auburn—like downtown Ventura and so many other downtowns across the United States—has reinvented itself successfully with breweries, restaurants, and entertainment venues. Many of these investors are native Auburnians who moved away for opportunity like I did—not a few of them, ironically, to Los Angeles—only to return because they missed the sense of community Auburn provided and the sense of authenticity they felt downtown. Half the historic downtown may be gone, but the other half is pretty great.

It has been a long journey for me since that day in the summer of 1974—from an eighteen-year-old boy covering his first urban renewal meeting to a sixty-five-year-old man who has been in the middle of urban development battles all over the country as a journalist and urban planner. But through it all, I have carried Auburn with me every minute of every day.

Many urban planners grow up in big cities and have a big-city perspective on what urban life should be like. But Auburn endowed me with a deep understanding that the benefits of urban life—close proximity to everything you need, the ability to walk and bike everywhere, a rich tapestry of everyday life—did not exist only in big cities. These benefits could exist in small towns too, so long as those towns had jobs

A downtown Auburn Street scene today *(Credit: Prison City Brewing)*

as well as people and could hang on to culture, entertainment, sports, and other activities indigenous to the place. When I saw these attributes begin to disappear in Auburn, it broke my heart and set me on a course to find them—and re-create them—in other small cities.

Today, it is more than satisfying to see these things still thriving to a certain extent in Auburn—and thriving and growing in small cities all across the country, including Ventura. Because without all these things, you can live in a place, but you are incomplete. With them, your town can be your house, as it was for both my father and for me.

CHAPTER 2

The Thinning Metropolis

When I was home in Upstate New York on our annual summer trip years ago, I delighted my ten-year-old daughter by taking her to the house I grew up in, which was built in 1924. I took special care to show her the layout of the backyards on the street. I had told her many times the story of how all us kids on the block used to go back and forth between other kids' houses by running through everybody's backyard—including the backyards of two families who didn't have any kids at home (and one of those backyards was the mayor's).

Even though this is one of my favorite stories and I had told it to her many times, my daughter didn't exactly believe me. The idea that it would even be physically possible to travel across a group of backyards was extremely foreign to her. Where she had grown up, in Southern California, the sky may be big, but the backyards are small and are separated from one another by shrubs, fences, or—most often—brick walls. But all the backyards on the street I grew up on were—and still are—separated by nothing at all.

And then there's the notion that an older, empty-nester couple, one of whom was the mayor, would let a bunch of little kids ram across their backyard all afternoon and evening also seemed unbelievable to her. If my daughter and her friends attempted to do that on our street in California, the whole neighborhood would be tied up in litigation for years.

There are important lessons to be learned by comparing thinning metropolises to thickening ones. Here, though, I am comparing two very specific types of places: the "thickening" cities of the arid West, which have grown up since World War II, and the "thinning" cities of Upstate New York, which saw their greatest growth between the opening of the Erie Canal in 1825 and the beginning of the Depression a century later.

To paint a picture of the urban pattern you see in Upstate New York versus what you see in California, forget about the differences in the landscape, green versus brown, trees versus scrub, the fact that California looks like the surface of the moon compared to Upstate. These differences are startling, but for our purposes they're irrelevant. Let's focus instead on the differences in the actual fabric of the built environment.

In Upstate, you typically see an older city, often dating to the nineteenth century, with an older housing stock contained in compact neighborhoods and, very often, a fine-grained urban fabric that, if replicated today, would be regarded as classic New Urbanism. On the edge of the city property you'll see housing subdivisions—some charming, some not, but none of these subdivisions will be very big— that were built sometime between the 1920s and the 1960s. Beyond that, in the "suburbs," you will usually find rows of postwar crackerboxes lined up along arterial roads or state highways, the lots getting bigger as you go farther out. Still farther, you will probably find a shopping center or two, as well as some newer subdivisions with fairly large lots. Then the suburbs will peter out into three- or five-acre lots—some with big houses, some with modest houses.

Past the suburbs, there might be a leftover farm or two, and then will come some nineteenth-century town of a thousand or so people, three blocks long along the highway, that has had its commercial base stripped away from it and now serves essentially as a bedroom suburb. Go past that and you will finally hit some farmhouses. Some will be in good shape, some will be rotting; some will actually house farmers, while others serve, in effect, as suburban housing.

In other words, what you will find is an extremely varied built environment, including compact towns, suburban sprawl, and rural areas, most of which was built so long ago that everything seems to be a part of the natural landscape. Except for some of the newer suburban subdivisions, everything feels deeply rooted in place.

Now, contrast this environment with the typical landscape of California—and think not of Los Angeles or San Francisco, but of the typical middle-sized suburban town of, say, a hundred thousand people that is endemic to the California landscape. In about half of them, there will be a tiny old downtown built as the commercial center of the town when it was one-tenth the size it is now, surrounded by a couple of older residential streets that may date back prior to the Great Depression. From there on out, you will see what we think of as suburban sprawl—mile after mile of large-scale suburban subdivisions, punctuated by business parks and shopping centers, all connected by arterial roads that seem, by themselves, to be wider than some entire towns around here. Whether built in the 1950s or the 1990s, these neighborhoods have a remarkably similar feel to them. Beyond the last wall of the last subdivision, you will find yourself in a "rural" area—usually either an industrial-scale farm or a wildland area essentially never touched by human manipulation.

To many people, this environment seems like suburban sprawl. That's because it's fairly new, it's large-scale, and it's uniform. But, interestingly enough, it's really not sprawl—not statistically anyway (because if we measure California's urban development, it's pretty dense) and certainly not compared to the area Upstate. For one thing, there's relatively little leapfrog development in the West these days. For another, the residential lot sizes are small—as small as twenty-five hundred to four thousand square feet in many places in California. Finally, there is no "petering out" into the countryside. The metropolis approaches the hinterland and overtakes it systematically at seven to ten units per acre.

Perhaps the difference between East and West can best be expressed through an anecdote recently related to me by a major developer's lawyer in Phoenix. He said his counterpart in Atlanta had tired of traffic and so had moved to downtown Atlanta from his eighty-acre farm on the outskirts of town. But, as the Phoenix guy pointed out, in the West, nobody lives on an eighty-acre farm, no matter how rich they are. There simply aren't any eighty-acre farms. Indeed, one of the oddest phenomena about the recent internet boom in Silicon Valley is that it has turned traditional assumptions about urban development on its head and highlighted the problems of "dense sprawl." The rich live close in, while the working class is forced into extremely long commutes. Why? Because going sixty miles out doesn't buy you more land. It just buys you a cheaper house at the same density.

I'm not saying that California and the West have a preferable form of urban development. There's a host of problems associated with growing in this fashion, as we all know. But I am saying that these areas use land extremely efficiently, and they are "thickening" in ways that are useful to think about, even in areas that seem to be terminally thinning, such as Upstate New York.

One place to start in thinking about this subject is to examine why these regional differences exist. That may sound like a silly question at first, because the most obvious reason simply has to do with demand. The West is adding population very quickly, and Upstate New York is not. If Upstate New York's population had been growing by a half-million people a year since the end of World War II, which happened in California, you would see that thickening there too.

All that is true enough, but that's not all there is to it. Once you really begin to plumb the similarities and the differences, some opportunities begin to emerge.

For example, population growth is not the only thing driving these differences. Dense sprawl in the West emerges from the interplay of a whole series of factors, including land ownership patterns and the cost of providing infrastructure, especially water and sewer service. Western cities are often hemmed in by federally owned land, and therefore have de facto urban growth boundaries around them. Las Vegas, for example, is completely encircled by federal land and will hit that boundary soon. That's why it's the most rapidly densifying city in the United States.

On the surface, it would appear, as the late Robert E. Lang of the University of Nevada, Las Vegas, liked to say, that the problem of sprawl is actually easier to solve in the West than in the East. The problem is not a lack of human activity but a lack of variety in distributing it across the landscape. In other words, the problem in the West is simply an urban design problem. The problem in the East, Lang argued, is much more difficult—and fundamentally different—because vast areas are characterized by low-density sprawl.

Ironically, however, one of the most important lessons of Western urbanization is that cheap, abundant land—the very commodity on which the myth of our national prosperity is based—is not the only driving force in shaping growth patterns. In fact, it may not even be the most important one. At least four other factors contribute to the "thickening" of the West, all of which can and will come into play in rethickening places like Upstate New York. The first is water. The second is, more generally, how public infrastructure systems are financed. The third is a general acceptance of urbanism by the American people.

Last—possibly the most powerful—is the changing profile of the American people themselves.

In some parts of the country, land may still be, for all practical purposes, infinite, but water is not. Water is a commodity that is already finite and getting more finite all the time in every part of the country. In the East, much of the "thinning" has relied on wells and septic systems. Conversely, in the West, much of the "thickening" has come about because wells and septic systems are not a viable form of urban development. In a water-poor environment, you have to hook onto public water and sewer systems to develop, which drives up the cost of infrastructure and creates pressure for density. We have already seen, in places like Long Island and New Jersey, how growth reaches its limits rather quickly if you're trying to create suburbia without public water and sewer systems.

Furthermore, once you start talking about public infrastructure, you quickly begin to talk about money and control on a regional basis. Almost everywhere, public infrastructure systems—especially water and sewer—are controlled or heavily influenced by the older, thinning cities that originally set them up. Yet, in the East, these cities are often remarkably ignorant of—or ineffective at dealing with—the way infrastructure funding affects growth.

Recently, the thinning city of Auburn, New York, where I grew up, finally reached an agreement with suburban towns on how to split the cost of upgrading the local wastewater treatment system, which the city owns but the towns use. As a result, the suburban towns are paying for a portion of the cost of both the upgrade and the system for the first time. Remarkably, in the past the central city footed the bill entirely, essentially subsidizing its own thinning.

Western cities have done a much better job of using infrastructure finance as leverage to shape surrounding communities. In Los Angeles, the central city still controls the regional sewage system and, to a considerable extent, the regional water system, and it has not been afraid to use this leverage, either to encourage suburban growth or to constrain it, depending on the circumstance. It's true that Western cities are younger and more able to exploit annexation laws to their advantage— what David Rusk calls the "elastic city"—but thinning Eastern cities must learn from Western cities to use infrastructure finance leverage to their advantage.

Thinning cities may also be able to take advantage of Americans everywhere appearing to have a new appreciation of urban places. As Robert Fishman has eloquently put it, US metropolitan areas are once again punctuated with "pockets of urbanism"—vibrant urban places where people work, shop, and sometimes live close to one another, often without much reliance on the car. This urbanism is different than the urbanism of a century ago in that it is diffuse within each metropolitan area and it is largely a function of lifestyle choice. Nevertheless, it is real.

This new "pockets of urbanism" phenomenon has been especially strong in Western cities, where each metropolitan area has many older, charming downtowns and where urbanism provides a respite from dense sprawl. Every place with a one-block Main Street is now thriving. In many parts of California, this phenomenon is driven in large part by the sheer hassle of traversing an enormous geographical area by car and the fact that "urbanism" represents an almost exotic approach to life— difference, compact, and manageable.

To be sure, it is difficult to transplant this view to a thinning metropolis, where virtually any one-block pocket of urbanism can be accessed by car in ten to twenty minutes. But in large part, the "pockets of urbanism" question is really the question of whether people are willing to choose a quaint older neighborhood instead of a half-acre lot. Increasingly, the answer—at least for a significant minority of the population—is yes.

Finally—and perhaps most importantly—the thinning metropolis can be revived and thickened in a positive way by the dramatic demographic change that has swept the country in the last generation. Once again, this phenomenon has swept the West—as well as a few large Eastern cities—first, but it will sooner or later provide an opportunity even for the smaller thinning cities in places like Upstate New York.

When the urban places of Upstate New York were dense and thriving in the industrial age, it was largely because of the lively and compact ethnic neighborhoods that had grown up in those cities, often in so-called factory-gate neighborhoods. There's a popular understanding that these neighborhoods existed in places like Boston, Chicago, and New York City, but we forget that they existed virtually everywhere that factory labor was in demand, even in small cities. These neighborhoods emerged quickly, they were very strong, and they lasted much longer than urban planners like me would have expected, simply because of ethnic loyalty and ethnic pride.

In Auburn, for example, the city had an Italian neighborhood, a Polish neighborhood, and a Ukrainian neighborhood. Each neighborhood had its turf, its restaurants, its Catholic parish, its social club, its schools, its shopping street, and its factory to provide a base of employment. The immigrants were the grandparents of the kids I went to high school with—and even though the grandchildren, my friends, were all going to college, the neighborhoods "held" because of ethnic loyalty and ethnic pride.

These neighborhoods were not perfect by any means. They were often crowded, and the worker housing, thrown up next to the factories around the time of World War I, was often lousy. But these neighborhoods worked in ways that we long to reproduce today. Well into the 1970s, it was still possible to live, shop, and work on Columbus Street in Auburn without ever leaving the neighborhood, getting into an automobile, or speaking any language except Italian. Many people who had the economic choice of leaving for a so-called better part of town—a better part of town being a mile or two away—chose nevertheless to stay. And this was in a town of thirty thousand people located in the dairy-farming country of Upstate New York.

With the great wave of immigration since the 1990s, we have begun to see these neighborhoods once again—especially in the West, where immigration from Asia and Latin America has been heavy. You see these neighborhoods all over the place in California. Virtually every older neighborhood with a stock of semi-affordable housing—the very neighborhoods that have emptied out in the Midwest, for example—are teeming with life. Yes, these neighborhoods are crowded, and the housing is often substandard. But in the California beach town of Ventura where I lived most of my adult life, it is possible to live, shop, and work on Ventura Avenue without ever leaving the neighborhood, getting into an automobile, or speaking any language except Spanish. In Los Angeles, in Orange County, in Phoenix, in Las Vegas, in Sacramento, and elsewhere, the same is true. The only thing that changes is the midday temperature and the language. As immigrant groups fan out across the United States to older cities everywhere, ethnic neighborhoods will be re-created and strengthened.

In places like Upstate New York, population stagnation may be inevitable. But the thinning phenomenon itself is not inevitable—not in a world where people are rediscovering the value of urbanism— where people are valuing place for the first time in a generation or two, discovering that limits, far from reducing opportunity, create more choices and more fiscal options. These are the lessons I learned intuitively as a boy in Auburn when I rode the bus with my mother down Genesee Street for the one-mile trip to the office of our dentist. They are the lessons I took West with me to California from Upstate New York, and remarkably, they are lessons California has learned as it has thickened. I hope they are lessons that can be brought back to places like Upstate New York in the years ahead as we confront the challenge of the thinning metropolis.

CHAPTER 3

The Garden Suburb and the New Urbanism

In the first chapter of *Home from Nowhere*, the New Urbanist critic James Howard Kunstler describes a scene in Seaside, Florida, in which the leading New Urbanist architects sit around and try to figure out why postwar American building and design had become, in Kunstler's words, "such an abysmal mess." The answer, Kunstler argued, is a version of "Victory Disease" after World War II: the war had been so cataclysmic that it caused Western civilization to forget much of its learning, and when the men who fought the war came home, they were so bored by everyday life that they drifted into a semi-alcoholic stupor and didn't really care about the world they were creating.

Kunstler is half-joking. But there is no question that these ideas, however good-naturedly put forth, arise from a persistent historical theory on the part of the New Urbanists: somehow American architects and planners fell into a kind of amnesia in the postwar years—maybe even in the late 1930s—from which they did not recover until sometime in the 1980s. Seduced by the car and by modern suburbia, they "forgot" all the universal truths about city design that had been practiced across cultures and over thousands of years and instead constructed a built environment that is, in Kunstler's hyperbolic words, "depressing, brutal, ugly, unhealthy, and spiritually degrading."

In other words, as far as the New Urbanists are concerned, something went terribly wrong during the suburban era, and they struggle against credibility to explain what happened. For example, contained in the New Urbanist manifesto, *Suburban Nation*, by the Miami New Urban duo of Andrés Duany and Elizabeth Plater-Zyberk along with DC-based New Urbanist Jeff Speck, is a lively assessment of the costs and consequences of sprawl, but its historical grounding, its explanations of causation, is less compelling that the authors' passionate quest for solutions.

Part of the reason they are so mystified by the development of postwar America is that the New Urbanists don't always understand the historical processes that created suburbia and stimulated interest in their own movement. This is not surprising: Despite their emphasis on "traditional" principles, the New Urbanists are practitioners, not historians, and they are working rapidly to meet current economic and political needs. But the debate over New Urbanism—which is often shrill or at least emotionally charged on all sides—would benefit from historical perspective.

When viewed in a historical context, New Urbanism can be properly understood as the continuation of a long-running intellectual struggle between two competing philosophies of urban design, best identified as the formal and the informal. Much of the friction between New Urbanists and other designers stems from the fact that the postwar American suburban tradition fell within the informal philosophy, while the core of New Urbanist design philosophy is formal in its approach.

In point of fact, most successful communities contain elements of both philosophies. The true test of New Urbanism will not be how purely it is created "on the ground." Rather, the test will be whether its most powerful ideas can be put into widespread use and combined with other powerful ideas, such as those from the informal tradition, to make better and more attractive communities.

At its root, New Urbanism is, as Vincent Scully once observed, really New Suburbanism because its original impetus was to create in systematic fashion the components required for a "better" suburb. In this regard, it emerges very much from the American "new town" tradition—an American adaptation of Ebenezer Howard's Garden City idea of 1900 or so.

The new town movement, and the garden suburbs that resulted, had Garden City intentions, but did not reflect a full realization of the Garden City principles. Garden Cities were designed to be self-contained, independent cities. But in a United States that was quickly becoming "metropolitan" in nature, such a self-contained community was virtually impossible to create. So the Garden City idea was transformed into the "garden suburb"—communities that embodied many of Howard's ideas but were not self-contained. According to the great urban planning author Lewis Mumford, the most essential parts of Howard's Garden Cities concept, "balance, variety, and manifoldness of urban function," were not implemented in garden suburbs, and thus, according to Mumford, they were not true garden cities: "nothing can be properly called a garden city that is not a complete and diversified urban community with its own industry." The American garden suburb movement, as distinct from Howard's Garden City idea, is best epitomized by Radburn, New Jersey, and the federal greenbelt towns dating from the 1930s.

Radburn and the federal greenbelt towns of the 1930s, which were designed based on the criteria of architect Clarence Stein, are true garden suburbs in the sense that they use naturalistic elements, rather than buildings and streets, as their focal point. In this sense, the garden suburb is akin to the quintessential suburban community of Riverside, Illinois, designed by Frederick Law Olmsted in 1868, which is based on the landscape architecture approach of manipulating nature to create an

Greenbelt, Maryland *(Credit: Fairchild Aerial Survey/Public Domain)*

artificial yet compelling naturalistic setting, responding to the inhuman nature of the crowded industrial city.

Radburn became a successful model for many reasons, but perhaps the most important was that in its design, Stein and his codesigner, Henry Wright, accepted the challenge of integrating the automobile into the community without surrendering the goal of allowing families and children to walk to everyday destinations. Many elements of the Stein/Wright garden suburb model were easily bastardized for mass consumption by the production-oriented real estate development industry in the United States.

Beginning in the late 1950s, when Jane Jacobs and William H. Whyte began writing about cities, an open rift emerged between these new defenders of crowded and untidy urban neighborhoods and the older advocates of Garden Cities and garden suburbs. Jacobs and Whyte were journalists acting as sociologists, observing what seemed to be working on the streets of New York. In the Jane Jacobs view, the critical design elements for successful neighborhoods were houses that face the street and a grid street system that ensured busy sidewalks—exactly the arguments made by the New Urbanists, in a more suburban context, almost forty years later. The reaction from Garden City advocates was strong. In 1965, Lewis Mumford wrote that "one would think that 'garden' was another name for 'open sewer.'" He also wrote an acidic article titled "Mother Jacobs' Home Remedies for Urban Cancer" in which he attacked traditional cities and their "ugliness, disorder, confusion."

Despite the criticism, from the beginning of their movement the New Urbanists embraced certain Garden City ideas, most particularly the neighborhood unit concept, with its carefully thought-out understanding of what civic and business activities should be integrated into the daily, pedestrian-oriented life of the neighborhood. But at the same time, however, the New Urbanists often explicitly rejected informal-style designs.

One interesting sidelight in the formal/informal debate within New Urbanism is that it has revived the design reputation of John Nolen, one of the most prolific early city planning consultants. Nolen is most frequently viewed as the P. T. Barnum of early twentieth-century city planning, a man who used his considerable public relations and networking skills to promote the idea of city planning as a profession. As a designer, though, Nolen has traditionally been derided as merely workmanlike compared to such contemporaries as Stein and Wright and the Olmsted brothers, who were Frederick Law Olmsted's sons.

Duany especially has used Nolen's work as a touchstone for his own design philosophy. Duany frequently points to Nolen's formalistic designs, his focus on prominent civic spaces, and his creative use of modified grid street systems. Duany is especially admiring of Nolen's famous design for Venice, Florida.

Thus, the New Urbanists dismiss Stein and embrace Nolen faster than one might expect. But such a dichotomy is rich with irony, because there is a great deal of overlap between Nolen and Stein that reveals the way in which the formal and informal design traditions are intertwined. It is these continuities, these common practices, rather than the differences, that contribute to a richer understanding of the invaluable role that both traditions have provided to American community design.

Nolen studied landscape architecture at Harvard, where he learned from his professor, Frederick Law Olmsted Jr., about the significance of using both formal and informal design traditions. Like Stein, Nolen designed one garden suburb—Mariemont, Ohio, outside Cincinnati, in the early 1920s—that was meant to serve as a national model for a suburban new town in a metropolitan area. Like his plan for Venice, which followed it by a few years, Nolen's plan for Mariemont incorporated both formal and informal elements. The civic and commercial spaces tend to reflect the formalistic tradition. Indeed, this part of the Mariemont plan (like the commercial and civic parts of the Venice plan) looks almost as if it could have been produced today by Duany and Plater-Zyberk's office. But the residential areas tend to reflect an Olmstedian informality.

Stein understood much better than Nolen the need to build new towns in the most economical manner possible. His approach emphasized servicing daily economic and community needs, such as shopping, rather than creating a grandiose sense of civic identity through site planning and public buildings. Stein spent a great deal of time, both at Radburn and with the Resettlement Administration, the New Deal agency that sponsored the federal greenbelt towns, on market studies and financial calculations.

It is also worth noting that, beginning in the latter half of the 1920s, auto traffic grew much more dramatically than any designer could have

Village of Mariemont, Ohio *(Credit: Mariemont Inn)*

predicted, raising questions about the viability of traditional town-center designs. Nolen's designs simply never took account of this fact, and many of his graceful town centers, such as Mariemont, quickly grew clogged with traffic. Stein, by contrast, designed Radburn as "a town for the motor age" and sought to separate cars and pedestrians as a way of allowing both to travel freely. In short, it was the suburb part of the garden suburb, as much as the garden part, that allowed the informal tradition to gain popularity.

Informal design prevailed over formal design beginning in the 1930s not because of a national amnesia or some kind of "Victory Disease," but because it was a design idea that seemed to address the needs of the time. In either pure or bastardized form, informal design could deliver houses more cheaply and accommodate auto traffic more efficiently than formal design, thus responding to what seemed to be the two most pressing problems at the time.

What was lost, of course, was an emphasis on the public realm, which stands at the center of the formal tradition. This formal public realm is represented by the structure and design of town centers to include grandiose civic buildings mixed with formal public meeting places. The formal public realm may also be referred to as the civic realm and is distinct from the informal public realm, which implies the manifestation of public and social gathering through greenbelts and other informal open space.

It is perhaps fitting that many of the Stein-influenced "new towns" of the 1960s are now building commercial centers that draw heavily on New Urbanism. In part, it is a happy consequence of one seemingly unhappy reality about American new towns. Metropolitan economics in the United States require the building of houses first so as to establish the market viability of a particular location. Shopping and office facilities are often built many years or even decades after the houses.

In both Reston, Virginia, and Valencia, California, Stein-style residential neighborhoods were built beginning in the 1960s, with informal architecture, naturalistic pedestrian "greenways," and other features clearly derived from Radburn and the greenbelt towns. Now that these communities are ripe for town centers, the developers are following the current trend of using New Urbanist–style formalism in their design.

This trend may suggest, as Nolen learned from Frederick Law Olmsted Jr. at the start of the twentieth century, that the formal and the informal fit together more successfully than many New Urbanists are willing to admit. The formal and the informal are the yin and yang of Garden City design. Both are required, and neither can be ignored. If New Urbanism is to fulfill its early promise of reestablishing successful formulas for American community design, and especially if it successfully navigates the transition from a suburban to a metropolitan landscape, the movement must understand the lessons of history about the valuable components of informalism and the power of commingling the two traditions rather than simply railing against informalism as impure.

CHAPTER 4

The Autocratic Citizen
of Philadelphia

By the time I actually met Ed Bacon, the legendary urban planner who died in 2005 at the age of ninety-five, he was already in his late eighties, cranky, and quirky. He had just read my book *The Reluctant Metropolis*, which reminded him that I had written a magazine article many years before that he had liked. He called me up out of the blue one day to discuss whether I should write—or help write—a biography of his life.

I was flattered that this legend of urban planning contacted me, and I agreed to meet with him on my next East Coast trip. Only later did I realize that I was not alone. Ed Bacon had flattered any number of writers over the years with exactly the same offer, and—at least at that time—no one had ever made a writing deal with him.

I first visited him at his Rittenhouse Square house in Philadelphia in the late 1990s. He proved to be chatty, charming, strongminded—even obsessive. The centerpiece of his house was on the third floor: an elaborate model of his vision for how to improve Independence Mall. Characteristically incensed that the city's planners had proposed a plan he didn't like, he built the model at his own expense to prove that his idea was better. He had fought the city's plan so hard that the planners of the day regarded him to be cantankerous almost to the point of being a gadfly. This was classic Bacon.

Bacon was born in Philadelphia in 1910 and was trained as an architect in the Beaux-Arts style at Cornell during the late 1920s. "I was there before the modernists arrived," he once told me. His zenith came during the 1950s and 1960s, when as executive director of the Philadelphia Planning Commission he engaged in the most successful urban revitalization efforts of the era, razing eight square blocks around Independence Hall to create a more formalistic setting and reviving the adjacent historical neighborhood of Society Hill in the process. He tore down the "Chinese Wall"—a large railroad bridge next to Philadelphia City Hall—to make room for the Penn Center office complex. And he rejected architect Louis Kahn's starkly modernist plan for the downtown.

Bacon had a way of coming across as naive, but he accomplished things no one so naive could have done. He was part of a political reform movement that pulled Philadelphia out of the machine era, and he helped rewrite the city charter in a way that gave the planning commission—and hence himself—more power than in almost any other city. He once told me that he did it by writing policies that would kick in far in the future, beyond the time horizon of all the politicians.

More than anything, however, he succeeded because he had an artist's vision and a monarch's will.

His vision was the city as the experience of moving through space—a path or a shaft—and most of his plans used this idea as the focal point. His idea of an implementation technique was to use the force of a will so strong that he seemed unable to separate Philadelphia from himself. The first chapter of his classic book *Design of Cities* is titled "The City as an Act of Will." In our first conversation at his house, he suggested that, having written a book about Los Angeles called *The Reluctant Metropolis*, I should now write a book about Philadelphia called *The Acquiescent Metropolis*.

"Acquiescent to whom?" I asked.

He looked at me in disbelief. "Why, to *me*, of course," he replied.

Tethered to such a strong personal vision and a strong personal will, Bacon did not seem to notice or care about the city's changing demographics or the growing significance of race and class in planning discussions, and eventually this made him seem old-fashioned and out of date. Bacon's decline began in the mid-1960s, when he went toe-to-toe with advocacy planners such as Paul Davidoff over the proposed construction of a freeway on the edge of Society Hill.

The freeway would have required the demolition of the Black neighborhood adjacent to increasingly tony Society Hill. Bacon, who taught at the University of Pennsylvania's architecture school, favored the freeway; Davidoff, who taught in the same university's planning school, opposed it. Davidoff won and Bacon lost, thus setting off a trend in advocacy planning and a corresponding decline in physical planning that lasted until the New Urbanists emerged twenty-five years later. (Another side effect of this battle was that my brother, who for many years ran a retail beer store on Bainbridge Street called Society Hill Beverage, stocked an extremely wide range of beers to meet the diverse market demand—Black and White, rich and poor—in the surrounding neighborhoods.)

Even today, almost all planning students read Davidoff's classic article, "Advocacy and Pluralism in Planning." But not very many of them read Bacon's *Design of Cities*. The New Urbanists revived Bacon's reputation to a certain extent; *Design of Cities* is on every New Urbanist reading list because Bacon's physical determinism and his formalistic design impulses jibe with New Urbanist thinking. Oddly, however, even the New Urbanists don't talk all that much about Bacon's accomplishments. I think that's because most of his urban design ideas, such as Penn Center, were implemented during the height of the modernist era and New Urbanists have always had a hard time admitting that good urban design can be created in a modernist style. But Penn Center *is* good—it's not perfect, but it's an excellent example of experiencing a city by moving through space, constructed at a time when such accomplishments were rare. It stands as a perpetual reminder that modernist architecture and bad urban design don't always go together.

I once asked Bacon why, given the force of his will and the breadth of his vision, he went along with modernism in revitalizing downtown Philadelphia. The great idealist gave me a surprisingly pragmatic answer. "I wouldn't have chosen it," he said, "but it was what I had available to me at the time."

I went to planning school at the height of the advocacy planning era and consequently gained almost no formal education in design. But I spent a lot of time in Philadelphia during the 1970s, before I moved to Los Angeles, and in a way I learned my urban design inside Bacon's mind. Many years later, when urbanism old and new came back into style, I was thankful that I had this education to fall back on.

CHAPTER 5

Having No Car but Plenty of Cars

When I moved to San Diego in 2013 without owning a car, people felt sorry for me. They offered me rides. They wondered where I would buy groceries. They asked me how I felt about being nature-deprived. They asked me how I could stand to ride the bus.

I would usually smile and nod and acknowledge what they were saying and tell them it really isn't so bad. I rarely told them that they were making a fundamental mistake: They were equating owning a car with using a car.

I belonged to Zipcar, and there were two Zipcars parked at all times in the parking garage in my apartment building—a Mini Cooper wagon and a Ford Escape SUV—that I could rent whenever I wanted. In fact, they were located closer to the elevator than my two eternally vacant parking spaces. I also belonged to the car-sharing company car2go (now part of Share Now). My smartphone could tell me when there were Smart FourTwo vehicles parked near my apartment, available for me to rent on a per-minute basis.

Avis Car Rental was located four blocks away. Sometimes I would rent a car for the weekend, although that seems awfully old-fashioned

car2go at a San Diego, California, trolley station
(Source: Thank You 21 Millions+ Views/Creative Commons)

these days. When I had to drive for work—my office was five blocks from my apartment—I had access to the city motor pool, which was located right downstairs in a parking lot outside my office building. I usually took a taxi to the airport (two miles away); from my apartment window, I could see whether there are any taxis waiting for a fare at the Doubletree Hotel across the street.

When I didn't know what else to do, I called Uber. There were generally a dozen Ubers within a few blocks of my apartment.

Cars? I had more cars than I knew what to do with. I used cars all the time, to go all kinds of places, and I was never without access to a car. My overall automobile cost was probably less than half of what it was when I owned a car because I usually paid for a car only when I was traveling in it, not when it was just parked somewhere.

I'm well aware that I was on the leading edge of this car-sharing idea and that the vast majority of people still don't have the same options because of where they live and work. But the fact that I did just fine without owning a car in a traditionally suburban place like San Diego suggested that something important was going on, at least in modern urban neighborhoods: Our complete reliance on a "monoculture" of owner-occupied automobiles has been augmented with a much more varied ecosystem that includes not just alternatives to driving, but many different ways to use a car.

The urban transportation infrastructure obviously also includes walking, bicycling, and rail and bus passenger service. (I could walk to the Santa Fe Depot in downtown San Diego from either my apartment or my office, making it easy for me to get to downtown Los Angeles without a car.) In California cities, these choices have not traditionally been "robust," as they say. But when they are augmented by the range of car-sharing options I had access to, the entire system becomes a much more powerful option. You can take a regular bus or train to a destination and then use a car-sharing service like Uber if you get stuck later in the evening when service is bad or nonexistent. Or you can use a car-sharing or a ride-hailing service as the "last-mile" solution to get to and from a rail stop. (This is part of the reason car-sharing services have been more successful in Los Angeles than even the vendors thought they would be, and in such a spread-out city, finding solutions to the last-mile problem is huge.)

Transportation infrastructure guru Dan Sturges once noted that any successful transportation system has to function like the vines that Tarzan uses in the jungle. Swinging from one vine isn't enough, he said. The next vine always has to be there, ready to grab, or else the whole system falls apart. All transportation systems work like that, but if they work well, we don't even notice. For example, we routinely take off on long car trips, confident that the infrastructure of well-placed gas stations will be available to us before we run out of gas. There is no government policy that ensures that this infrastructure exists; the private market has taken care of it.

The same is true for car sharing. The more options we have, the more powerful the system becomes. We can move about the city using many of these options, confident that the next swinging vine will always be there.

Obviously, many people—especially in suburban locations—will always have activity patterns that will require them to own their own cars, drive them everywhere, and leave them parked most of the time. But for even semi-urban locations—such as old close-in single-family neighborhoods adjacent to commercial corridors—the swinging vine option is pretty viable. The swinging vines can help transform these neighborhoods much faster than public transit alone ever could do. And success is likely to feed on itself. The more people use these options, the less parking these neighborhoods will need. Heavy use of Uber or Lyft cars, which are constantly circling around, reduces the need for parking. But research also suggests that one car2go or Zipcar—which the user has to park somewhere—has a similar impact because as a short-term rental car it will be driven more and parked less. Plus you can park two car2go smart cars in one parking space. When less parking is needed, more land can be devoted to new buildings, which means a greater concentration of both people and destinations in one place, which means even less need for parking and greater opportunities for using the swinging vine.

From this perspective, the traditional suburban model seems pretty archaic—and expensive. Cars that are parked virtually all the time, at great expense to their owners? Huge amounts of land devoted to parking that could be devoted to more profitable or more human-scale uses? How rigid! How inflexible! How expensive! How twentieth-century!

Obviously, this suburban model will be with us for a long time because so many people live and work in suburban locations. And huge numbers of people will continue to make the suburban choice. often with long commutes. They will then have little choice but to own their own cars, drive them everywhere they go, and park them virtually all the time. But for urban and semi-urban neighborhoods, car sharing seems like an almost miraculous way out of the conflict between density and driving. In those neighborhoods, the ongoing and often inevitable transition away from the suburban model will become more viable, cheaper, and much easier to plan for.

CHAPTER 6

Tom Hayden's Cars

On the day after Tom Hayden died in Santa Monica in 2016, I went on a tour of new urban development near stations along the Expo Line, the then-new light-rail line that connects Santa Monica to Downtown Los Angeles. It was a bit of a homecoming for me: my life in Southern California began and ended within spitting distance of that line, and despite all my years in Ventura, so much of what went on in between was tangled up with Los Angeles's Westside.

The tour made me realize how much has changed on the Westside— even in the last few years, but certainly since I had first met Hayden thirty-five years earlier. Two things struck me.

The first—especially at our first stop at the Culver City station—is the weird and ever-changing relationship between the Westside and the car. Yes, the Westside is rich and hip, and yes, ridership on the Expo Line was exploding. Nevertheless, cars were littered everywhere on the Westside, and folks there are still obsessed with moving them and storing them.

The second—especially at our last stop at Bergamot Station in Santa Monica—is how thoroughly the Hayden-era model of urban development, if you want to call it that, was being rejected by the people there. Hayden was the godfather of the left-wing faction that took over Santa Monica on a rent control platform in 1981, and he represented the Westside in Sacramento for almost twenty years. For decades, the deal for developers in Santa Monica was simple: we'll give you what you want if we can extract enough community benefits from you. But the debacle at Bergamot—including the city council's decision to rescind prior approval of a big mixed-use project and the subsequent slow-growth measure on the ballot that fall—made it clear that this deal wouldn't work anymore on the Westside.

If you add these two things together, you get a pretty interesting picture of how the Westside had evolved and how much it struggled with being a victim of its own success—as well as how much the Westside slid back into twentieth-century thinking when the going got tough.

Our first stop was at the Culver City station, near Helms Bakery. Culver City is doing a great job of station-area planning, and the resulting district is going to be an excellent walkable neighborhood with strong connections to downtown Culver City. But the most amusing part of our visit there was the automated parking garage at the old Helms Bakery, whose owners had lovingly transformed into modern office and retail space.

The parking garage is indeed impressive. Cars are automatically parked using a lift and moved around the garage based on the established patterns of the drivers. If you don't use your car during the day, it gets shuffled to the back; if you are in and out, it stays in the front. Your car will be gradually moved closer to the exit as it gets closer to the time you typically leave work. Retrieving a car, even from an upper floor, takes a matter of seconds.

But as I watched and listened, I kept thinking that this must have been how IBM talked about how great the Selectric typewriter was right before the personal computer was invented. Yes, the Helms garage is all about efficiency—but it's about *storing* and *retrieving* cars efficiently. Today, the buzz in urban circles worldwide is about Uber, car sharing, and autonomous cars—that is, *using* cars more efficiently so that you don't need to store or retrieve them in the first place.

In New York and San Francisco today, you are how you ride or where you go. On the Westside, you are still *what* you drive—so twentieth century. That was part of the reason it was refreshing to move on to the next stop, the Bundy Station on the Expo Line and the adjacent Martin Cadillac dealership.

When I first moved to Los Angeles in the early 1980s, I lived within walking distance of the Martin Cadillac dealership at Olympic and Bundy—not that you would have wanted to actually walk to Martin Cadillac in those days. (Take my word for it: then, as now, I didn't own a car.) After almost fifty years on this five-acre site, Martin Cadillac will soon give way to a large mixed-use development.

The visit was a good reminder that car dealers are often sitting on the best properties in transit-rich neighborhoods, and the clever ones are smart enough to realize that as they become retail dinosaurs, real estate is their biggest asset. The Bundy stop is still much an amenity desert, but between the Expo Line and the big office buildings nearby, which date back to the '80s, the pedestrian traffic is respectable. At lunchtime that day I saw about thirty people walking around at Olympic and Bundy, an intersection that features not only Martin Cadillac, but a bunch of gas stations and convenience stores.

One stop to the west is Bergamot Station, which features a combination of hip galleries and other arts businesses, high-end creative office businesses located in old industrial buildings, and traffic-spewing office towers from the 1980s. My life in Los Angeles may have begun down the street near Martin Cadillac, but it ended here thirty-two years later, when I was one of the principals in charge of the Bergamot Area Plan for the firm now known as PlaceWorks. And I do mean ended, because that plan—and some of the development projects that might have been built near the station—suffered the most ignominious fate of any planning effort in Southern California in recent memory. With it died the Hayden-era idea of soaking the developers to get social goods, which has apparently been replaced by the retro planning idea that doing nothing is usually better than doing something.

The plan was supposed to build on Santa Monica's vaunted 2010 Land Use and Circulation Element (LUCE). The LUCE, which supposedly had broad public support, was built on the concept of "tiers"—the idea that developers could get higher tiers of density in exchange for providing more community benefits. The LUCE was the ultimate manifestation of the Hayden-era development-for-goodies formula that was developed by the first progressive leaders in Santa Monica in the 1980s: Sure, we'll give you the density for whatever the market is demanding (office, housing, retail), so long as you give us lots of social benefits in return. This was radical thinking back then, when most people's idea of urban planning activism was to shut down new development. And even though Hayden and his buddies had a reputation for being socialists, it requires a deft understanding of capitalism to make this idea work. You have to know just how hard to squeeze the developers so that you still get the goodies and the developers don't go away.

Over time, as capitalism took over the Westside, the argument for a bigger squeeze only increased. Today in Santa Monica, the market is so strong that developers will, quite literally, pay almost any price for entitlements.

But that isn't what happened when a major developer proposed a major mixed-use project on Olympic Boulevard right across the street from Bergamot Station. The project was arguably not the best designed project ever, although it dramatically improved pedestrian connectivity and publicly available open space in the area. Nor, apparently, did the developer do an especially good job selling it to the neighbors. The bottom line was that just before the 2014 local election, the city council members up for reelection rescinded approval of the development agreement, apparently to avoid losing their seats. Subsequently, they also backed off a lot of the good stuff contained in the LUCE.

They did save their own skins, at least for a while, but at a cost. The developer sold the land and the existing Paper Mate factory was retrofitted—meaning that there is still a twelve-hundred-foot wall along Olympic Boulevard and no sidewalk. Yes, the latest biggest project on Olympic Boulevard went away. But so did all the goodies. And so, by the way, did a lot developers who could have been squeezed.

Meanwhile, the defeat of the mixed-use project infected the entire Bergamot plan, and many of the other things that would have created better connectivity and a mixture of activities went out of the plan. The status quo, however imperfect, was judged to be better than anything new.

In a certain way, you can't blame Santa Monica's residents for taking such an anti-growth attitude. After all, they've been hammered with job-related traffic for thirty years. But in rejecting dense twenty-first-century mixed-use growth, they are stuck with twentieth-century problems, like no sidewalks, no connectivity, and even no restaurants. They also have no affordable housing and none of the other things that the Hayden-era activists in Santa Monica wanted, because they are stuck with the twentieth-century solution of simply retaining the status quo.

So even as Hayden—perhaps the prototypical twentieth-century lefty intellectual—slipped away in a hospital a short distance away, the section of Los Angeles that he loved remained mired in twentieth-century thinking. Unfortunately, it's not the twentieth century anymore.

CHAPTER 7
Talk City

Late in 2006, not long before I announced that I was running for re-election to the Ventura City Council, I decided to start writing a blog. Most people thought it was just a campaign stunt, but I had a different idea in mind: I wanted to make sure my constituents understood the reasoning behind my votes, and the time and space to do that explaining simply wasn't available during the high-profile, high-pressure Monday night council meetings.

At first I tried to write a blog every Tuesday morning, picking up whatever we had dealt with the night before as my topic. At the time, the topic was often some development project or a land use plan, which was usually the most contentious issue on the agenda and also fell within my area of professional expertise as a city planner. Indeed, improving the planning and development situation in Ventura was the main reason I ran for office in the first place. It wasn't long, however, before both the topics and the nature of the blog began to change.

When the economy crashed in 2008, the focus of the city council's work shifted away from managing growth and development toward—not to mince words—keeping the city solvent as our revenue dropped. As was the case throughout the United States, the whole political milieu in Ventura became much more sharp-edged and acrimonious. At the same time, I moved up to a leadership position in Ventura, serving as deputy mayor and mayor in the four years of my second term. (Typical of smaller California cities, mayor and deputy mayor are not separately elected in Ventura but rather chosen by the city council from among its members for two-year terms.) For all these reasons, the blog moved away from explaining how I had voted toward defending what we were doing.

Maybe because the meetings themselves were so bruising—and therefore not always easy to re-live the next morning—I also found myself wanting to move beyond the city council's work and write about a much broader range of topics about our community. I wrote about how our downtown parking system was actually working. I wrote about how the death of a beloved twenty-year-old affected our entire community. I wrote about how artists enriched our lives.

In most ways, Ventura is a typical Southern California beach town. It's a pretty and historic working-class oil town sixty miles northwest of Los Angeles, a regionally important surf spot, one of California's original mission towns, and the seat of the Ventura County government. It's gradually becoming a suburb of uber-expensive Santa Barbara and, to a lesser extent, uber-huge Los Angeles. My family moved to Ventura in the 1980s because it seemed like a good place for our kids to grow up, and it was. Even today, Ventura has an unusually robust community life, where people know one another many different ways—through parent-teacher organizations, soccer leagues, senior centers, community orchestras, art programs, environmental organizations, and all kinds of other activities.

But from the beginning I could see that Ventura had a lively, colorful, and sharp-elbowed political scene. The police and fire unions, the chamber of commerce, the developers, the local anti-growth environmentalists—all were in constant battle with one another. The "Letters to the Editor" page of the local newspaper was immensely entertaining reading. The gadflies were far more interesting in Ventura than any-where else I could recall, led—if you could call it that—by a voluntarily homeless man who wore a black cape, a cycling cap, and a Wyatt Earp mustache and bicycled around town carrying his laptop computer. (He ran and lost for the city council every time out.)

The city council met in an elegant 1912 Beaux-Arts former court-house, in the very room where the last woman ever executed in Califor-nia had once been tried for the murder of her pregnant daughter-in-law. Outbursts had become so disruptive at city council meetings that applause had been banned and replaced with the American Sign Lan-guage version of applause instead—a kind of wiggly hand-waving above the head that made it seem as though the city council chambers had just been infected by a stadium wave. In some ways, it was typical small-town politics; in other ways, it was as high pressure and ruthless as a presidential campaign.

I got involved in civic life in Ventura in the late 1990s, when I was appointed to the city's library commission and, shortly thereafter, when the city council asked me to chair a thirty-nine-member stakeholder committee charged with creating a common vision for the future of Ventura. Although most people loved Ventura's historic, small-town-by-the-sea-near-LA environment, it had become very hard for people to agree on much of anything else.

Although Ventura often seemed paralyzed by the political diversity of its residents, I grew to love practically everybody who was involved in politics or civic life. Rarely did they fit into a neat political box. Surfing environmentalists were often hard-core libertarians as well. The evan-gelical pastors, though extremely conservative on most political issues, had a strong sense of social justice and were committed to helping the homeless, single mothers with small children, and others who were hav-ing a hard time.

And you never knew where help would come from next. One Sunday after a service at the local Unitarian Universalist Church, I was approached by a man in his thirties wearing all-black clothing and sporting several tattoos. He was accompanied by his wife and daughter, both of whom wore dark, heavy makeup and were likewise dressed all in black.

"Mayor Fulton," he said, "I just wanted to say we love what you're doing. We are so excited about where Ventura is going."

I thanked him in a perfunctory way, and he added, "We were wondering—how can the *Goth* community get more involved?"

Despite this passion, political diversity, and quirky sense of commitment, Venturans had a deeply conflicted view of their own government. On the one hand, people usually expected the city to do everything. It was an old-fashioned "full-service" city, which provided all services (police, fire, parks, water, and sewer), and very often it was the only local institution big enough and with enough revenue to initiate any large-scale undertaking. On the other hand, most people didn't vote in local elections, they were deeply skeptical of the city government's competence, and they regularly voted down tax increases and tied the city's hands on policy decisions via other ballot initiatives.

Sometimes we couldn't even agree on what to call our city. The official name is San Buenaventura, named for the mission, which was in turn named for St. Bonaventure, the thirteenth-century Catholic saint. (St. Bonaventure was a Franciscan, as was Father Junipero Serra, father of the California mission system.) That name had been shortened to "Ventura" in the nineteenth century, supposedly because the full name was too long to fit on the railroad schedules. Yet as a city we never quite decided what to call ourselves—even our wayfinding signs said Ventura in some locations and San Buenaventura in others. In the middle of a heated debate on this topic one night, the longtime city council member said, "We should use San Buenaventura on all our signs so everybody knows they're in Ventura."

I ran in 2003 largely as a follow-up to the community visioning effort and also because as a city planner with a statewide reputation I felt I could help heal the scars from the growth wars and help the city set a new course of responsible and high-quality development. I was worried that in the long run Ventura could become nothing more than a tourist, retirement, and commuter town and gradually lose its character.

Although I ran in part as an environmentalist—it was hard to get elected in Ventura *without* being an environmentalist—over time I settled on two themes for my time in elected office: improving the quality of life in Ventura and creating enduring prosperity. These were not easy themes to translate into action. The first theme was, of course, subject to everybody's definition of quality of life. Improving one person's quality of life often involves harming somebody else's—or at least many people think so. The second theme of creating enduring prosperity often means picking your spots and not giving somebody what they wanted in the short term. As I often said, just because something was in the short-term financial interest of some landowner didn't mean it was in the long-term economic interest of the city and its residents.

During my first term, pursuing these objectives was difficult but not impossible. A reform movement had emerged in my field of urban planning—commonly known in those days as "smart growth"—which focused not on the quantity of new development but the quality and geographical distribution of that development. We were able to use some of these ideas to break the traditional gridlock over growth by adopting a new general plan, redoing some of our codes, and approving many new development projects, especially in our downtown. We also hired smart growth advocate Rick Cole, a legendary former mayor of Pasadena, as our city manager. (Cole went on to serve as a deputy mayor to Los Angeles Mayor Eric Garcetti and city manager of Santa Monica. He also wrote the foreword to this book.) Unfortunately, few of those projects were ever built because of the Great Recession, which began in 2007.

During my second term—which coincided with the Great Recession—it was almost impossible to focus on improving anything, especially in the long term. We were confronted every day with just trying to keep our head above water financially and keeping the city solvent.

During the recession—when I served as deputy mayor and mayor—I was surprised at how hard it was to truly engage my constituents and overcome the general skepticism about our financial situation, the limits on our ability to do things, and even whether we were telling the truth. I also came to see how hard it was to move past the desire to talk about everything forever in preference to actually doing things. As we used to say at city council meetings, "Everything has been said, but not everybody has had the chance to say it." I had no problem with endless talk if it led to a consensus to act. Often, however, I was frustrated when the talk seemed to be an end in itself and served as a process designed to reach a consensus to do nothing. Because doing nothing, in my opinion, was a choice about how to proceed—and not always a good one.

One thing about local politics in California—especially in coastal towns where ballot measures are the norm—is that the voters are all over you in a way that they usually aren't when you are in some higher elected office. During my time on the city council, we put a sales tax increase on the ballot twice. Both tax increases failed. Partly they failed because it was hard to explain why California's complicated fiscal system put a city like Ventura at a disadvantage, and partly it was because we couldn't overcome the general belief that somehow or other we were wasting a lot of money. (One of the sales tax measures required a two-thirds vote; it "failed" with 62 percent.)

We were also wrestling constantly with ballot measures on other issues; in California, residents can place any proposed legislation on the ballot. During my time, we had to deal with a ballot to create a committee that would have usurped the elected officials' power, enacted an ordinance trying to keep Walmart out of town, and overturned the city council's decision (after several years of discussion) to put parking meters on Main Street downtown. Plus I had to contend with an attempt to recall me because I had facilitated the closure of a library during the recession.

None of these measures passed. Some of them never made it to the ballot. But all of them required an enormous amount of attention at times when we were trying to figure out how to keep the city solvent during the worst recession in seventy years. And it was very difficult to help our constituents see what a tough spot the city was in—not just because they were pressuring us on this or that issue, but because California's peculiar and complicated system of local government finance was almost impossible to explain to the average person.

Most constituents, for example, believed that we got plenty of money from the property taxes they paid. In fact, because of the Proposition 13 property tax limitation, we didn't get much at all. Longtime homeowners paid very little tax, and the city got only a small portion of what they did pay. (Most of the money went to the county and the school district.) Yet those longtime homeowners were often the loudest voices to criticize us when we had to cut services because of declining revenue during the recession.

Especially during the recession, our constituents were understandably focused on pressuring us to maintain their favorite city activity or service, but they often had a hard time coming to terms with the tradeoffs required to do so. During the recession, I had conversations with constituents almost every day who told me that we shouldn't cut their—pick one—library service/fire station/park/senior citizen program. When I would ask them what we should cut instead, their typical reaction was, "I don't know. That's your job."

On top of that, even though everybody in Talk City had lots of opinions, not very many of them voted. Turnout was below 30 percent in both off-year elections in which I ran. (Voters have since approved a charter amendment to move the municipal election to even years.) As I always used to say, whenever I spoke to a group of citizens, most of the people in the room had not voted for me—or against me. How could the people who lived in Ventura really feel invested in what we did at city hall if they hadn't even participated in deciding who was sitting on the dais?

In the end, like all politicians, I got less done than I had hoped. I felt penned in between the expectations of my constituents—as well as my own expectations, for that matter—and our ability to meet those expectations. In retrospect, I would have done a lot of things differently. I would have worked harder to try to keep our branch library open in 2010—but at the time, there was no existing pot of money we could use and no political consensus to raise taxes. I probably wouldn't have increased the firefighters pensions in 2008—but at the time, the fullness of the economic downturn wasn't entirely clear.

It wasn't just that the city didn't have enough money, although that was a big part of it during my second term. It was also partly because, as is often the case in politics, in the short term doing nothing is often easier than doing something, no matter what the long-term consequences might be. And it was partly because navigating myriad constituencies toward a desired outcome during tough economic times was much harder than I ever imagined.

Yes, in some ways Ventura seemed worse off when I left office in 2011 than when I was elected in 2003. That was almost inevitable given the budget situation. But over the course of time we managed to restore at least some transparency and credibility to the city government, and we healed many of the scars that had been left by thirty years of growth wars. In retrospect, the Great Recession was also a time of great innovation. Ventura implemented new ways to provide police and fire service. We found new ways to partner with nonprofit organizations to provide social services and cultural programs. And we got through the entire recession with a good credit rating while laying off only two people.

And even in the depths of the recession, I could tell that the people of Ventura—like people in other cities—were becoming more appreciative of and excited about Ventura as a city. Not just as a municipal government that provides them with services, but as a place that sustains and nurtures them.

Ventura's distinctive historic downtown did not go downhill during the recession; in fact, it did better than the mall. Although most of the development projects we considered in those days never got built, the ones that did were important: the first single-family housing development in a generation that contained a neighborhood park; several affordable housing projects, built at a time when prices were going up and incomes were not; a new hospital; and an expanded museum. All these things made Ventura better as a city and as a place.

And especially because of the hard times, I came to appreciate more than ever what a strong sense of community Ventura had. It was a place people identified with, and even though that quality made political debate difficult at times, it also created a remarkable strength and resiliency that has always helped Ventura thrive. As I said repeatedly during my time in office, Ventura can do things that other cities just can't do. I always knew this—it was part of the reason we moved to Ventura in the first place—but I came to appreciate it more than ever before while I was in office and especially in those difficult last couple of years.

After I left office, I first traveled the United States as an advocate for smart growth development, then served as a big-city planning director, and then headed a university-based urban think tank. All these experiences have only strengthened my belief in the future of Ventura—and all cities. Despite financial struggles, cities continue to serve as effective providers of basic services, incubators of social and economic innovation, and strong, well-rounded places for people to live and grow.

CHAPTER 8

Why I'm Scared to Walk in Houston

I still remember the exact moment when I first became scared as a pedestrian in Houston. It was a Saturday afternoon in 2017, and I was at the intersection of Waugh Drive and West Dallas Street—two fast-moving, four-lane arterials in the Montrose district. I was headed south across West Dallas. When the traffic light changed, I got the walk signal and stepped off the curb. First, a car making a right turn from southbound Waugh onto westbound West Dallas cut me off by a foot or two. Then a car making a left turn from northbound Waugh onto westbound West Dallas did the same.

In other words, walking legally in a crosswalk where I had the right-of-way, I almost got hit twice by separate fast-moving cars turning from opposite directions across my crosswalk. When I finally made it to the other side of the street, I was shaking. I haven't been the same since.

I have been a pedestrian my whole life—visual impairment has caused me to walk more, ride transit more often, and drive less than the average person—but walking in Houston has changed me in a way I never thought was possible. I am scared all the time and fatalistic about my chances. More important, I fear for the future of this great city. Because as it grows and changes, especially in an era of self-driving cars, most of us will wind up interacting with busy city streets as pedestrians (and maybe as bicyclists too) far more than we do now. And that requires a profound change in our motoring culture—not just from motorists themselves, but also from the authorities—that so far isn't happening.

When a bicyclist was killed by a dump truck at the corner of Sunset Boulevard and Main Street—the second bicycling member of the Rice University community to be killed at that intersection in an eighteen-month period—police officials immediately told reporters to warn bicyclists that when they are crossing the street in a crosswalk they should walk their bikes or else they will be violating the law. A number of people—including the leadership of BikeHouston, a policy and advocacy group—actually disputed this interpretation of the law, but whatever the law, the attitude is striking.

Think about it: A dump truck turned right across a crosswalk and killed a bicyclist who was traveling straight ahead. The cops immediately warned bicyclists that they must walk their bikes and look out for vehicles. The cops did *not* warn drivers that when they are turning into a crosswalk, they might want to look to see if there is anybody there.

This kind of blaming and shaming pedestrians and bicyclists is not new. It dates to the 1920s when cities in the United States first passed jaywalking laws—essentially criminalizing the act of walking and relieving motorists of the responsibility to be careful. But the twenty-first-century city is going to be a very different place to move around in, and it's time for Houston—along with other cities—to recognize that times have changed.

Walking in most cities is unpleasant. I lived for many years in and around Los Angeles—a very car-centric place—and walking there was tough (although it's gotten better). But the experience of walking in Houston is unlike anything I have ever experienced.

Graphic "Watch for Cars" sign in Houston *(Credit: William Fulton)*

Part of it is simply that Houston motorists are not accustomed to thinking there might be pedestrians, so they don't look for them. And part of it is that motorists are human: emotional, distracted, often focused on something else, a problem that has gotten worse in recent years. But to a surprising extent motorists in Houston simply show a willful disrespect for pedestrians.

Almost every day as I walk around the city, drivers cut me off or simply drive around me because they don't want to wait. Many are driving with one hand, the other holding a cell phone up against their ear. On a half-dozen occasions, I have come up to an intersection where I have the right-of-way, started to cross the street, and looked straight into the eyes of a driver looking right back at me. Each time, after looking at me while I approach the car, the driver has simply cut me off. As a result of these experiences, I've gotten much more hard-edged as a pedestrian. I try to make eye contact, but it's not a kind or humane eye contact. It's a glaring, don't-mess-with-me eye contact. Walking in Houston has, in a certain way, turned me into a New Yorker.

Many traffic engineers—especially in a place like Houston—hold the view that the solution is that there should basically be no pedestrians or bicyclists. They believe that for everybody to be safe, everybody should be encapsulated in a personal vehicle. Based on my personal experience, more than a few Houston motorists seem to hold that view. This makes engineering sense in a weird, narrow way, but it's basically a twentieth-century suburban point of view. It's not going to work in twenty-first-century Houston.

Pedestrian on a busy arterial in Houston, Texas
(Source: Google maps/Kinder Institute Urban Edge)

For one thing, more and more people cannot afford cars due to low wages. According to the US Census Bureau, there are 100,000 households in Harris County that have no vehicle at all and there are more than 140,000 households that have two people—presumably adults— and only one vehicle. There are countless other households where multiple adults must share vehicles because of their economic circumstances and have to rely either on public transportation or a complicated family system of chauffeuring and carpooling. As more and more people of modest means get displaced from the central city to the suburbs by gentrification—and farther away from bus lines—this problem is only going to get worse.

At the same time, it's simply not possible to simultaneously expect to live in a city (1) that is prosperous and growing, (2) where everybody travels in a personal vehicle, and (3) where there is no traffic congestion. Among these three factors, sooner or later something has to give. And that something will probably be the use of the personal vehicle, at least as we know it now, which means more of us will be out on the streets.

Many people believe that ride-hailing services like Uber and Lyft and self-driving cars will magically solve all these problems—especially for people like me, who have some impairment that prevents them from driving like everybody else. And it's true that ride-hailing services are a boon to people like me who can afford them. But ride-hailing services and self-driving cars all by themselves won't solve the affordability problem for low-wage workers. Nobody making $9 an hour is going to pay $8 or $10 or $15 for an Uber ride instead of $1.25 for an inconvenient Metro bus ride—or nothing for a dangerous bicycle commute. Nor will such services solve congestion, meaning not everyone will use them even if they can afford them. No matter how good ride-hailing services and self-driving cars become, it will still be cheaper and faster to get out of, for example, the Texas Medical Center in the afternoon on a Red Line light-rail train than in a personal vehicle of any kind—just as it is now. Thousands of middle-class people who work at the Med Center ride the train because they understand this.

Most important, though, is that ride-hailing services—and, eventually, self-driving cars—are not a substitute for suburban-style personal transportation. That means more people will have a different type of relationship to the city around them.

In all likelihood, all these services—fixed-rail transit, buses, ride-hailing services, pooled self-driving cars, bicycling, and even walking short distances through city streets—will work together along with personal vehicles to create a more nimble and flexible transportation system that responds to people's needs in twenty-first-century Houston, especially in the central parts of the city. As this more varied transportation system emerges, one eternal truism will become more obvious: Everybody begins and ends every trip as a pedestrian. A lot more people will be exposed—as I am now—to the dangers of walking amid city traffic. So we all have a stake in making the city safer for pedestrians, because we are all pedestrians—and with the coming of self-driving vehicles, we will all be pedestrians more often than we are now.

After the fatal collision at Sunset and Main, my pal Raj Mankad wrote a powerful op-ed in the *Houston Chronicle* saying there was no point in writing powerful op-eds about pedestrian and bicycle safety in Houston because there is no hope for improvement. I hope he is wrong, but I am afraid he is right. Sooner or later, I'll get struck by a vehicle in this town. It's inevitable. I can only hope that when this collision happens it will be with a small car, not a dump truck; that the vehicle will be going slow, not fast; that I will live, not die; and that cops don't tell Melanie Lawson of Channel 13 that it was probably my fault. Until Houston finally decides to get serious about changing its car culture, those are the choices that I—and thousands of other Houstonians—face.

CHAPTER 9

My Favorite Street

My favorite street is closed to cars at the moment. But not to people. And that's just fine with me.

In the midst of the COVID-19 pandemic, the Ventura City Council extended what is technically known as the Temporary Outdoor Business Expansion Program—more popularly known as Main Street Moves. Simply put, because indoor dining was prohibited in California, Main Street in downtown Ventura was blocked off to cars so that restaurants could put tables out on the street.

Main Street Moves is a whopping success, and it shows what makes a truly great street: It's flexible. It's able to bend to the demands of the moment, rather than rigidly serving one purpose at all times.

I have driven Main Street thousands of times. I have also walked it, biked it, and ridden a bus along it more times than I can count. But along Main Street, I've also lit Christmas trees, twirled in fake snow, eaten tornado potatoes, accompanied the police as they sorted out a marital dispute, shot the breeze with homeless people, gotten into an argument with angry Tea Partiers over the constitutionality of the parking meters, watched my bleary-eyed daughter walk down Main Street

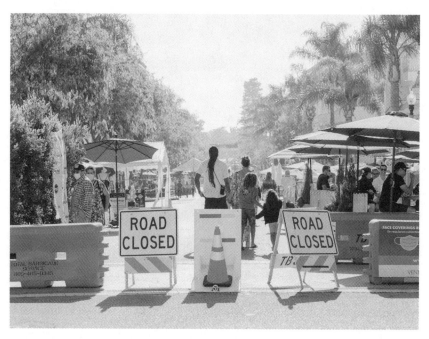

Main Street, Ventura, California, set up for outdoor dining during the COVID-19 pandemic *(Credit: Gary Brink)*

to middle school with a giant Starbucks cup in her hand, dined on just about every type of food you could imagine, gotten into more than one fight with a girlfriend, ridden in a dozen or so parades, observed the police chief in a friendly conversation with the head of our local Hells Angels chapter, sat in on an Italian class at a sidewalk café that gradually turned into a discussion group about politics, and lived for a while in a big blue Victorian on Main Street.

Through all these experiences—much more so than through the thousands of times I have driven down the street—Main Street in downtown Ventura has become a part of me. Partly, of course, this is an emotional connection that was established over twenty-five years of participating in life in Ventura. But mostly it's because Main Street is used not just for cars but to help people actually live—and celebrate—life.

There's a big debate in urban planning these days about what streets are for. Are they simply to move cars, which is how most people travel, as fast as possible? Or are they meant to serve a variety of purposes: moving pedestrians, bicyclists, and people on public transit and acting as a kind of backdrop for life, which require that cars be slowed down or even removed in some cases? Not long ago, for example, San Francisco removed all cars from Market Street, as New York did on 14th Street.

The answer to the question of what a street is for is, "It depends." Under ordinary circumstances, you can use downtown Ventura's Main Street to drive from one place to another, although you'd be going pretty slow and it would probably take a while. If you want to get somewhere in a hurry, there are alternatives, including the Highway 101 freeway three blocks away. But as my friend Roger Millar, now secretary of transportation in Washington State, likes to say, if you don't want traffic engineers to flatten your town in an attempt to move cars, they have to think of it as a *destination*, not a place people pass through. That's what makes Main Street my favorite street: It's a destination—a place people go.

The key to making Main Street a destination is *flexibility*—the ability to speed traffic up, slow it down, or even just close it to traffic altogether to serve the community's needs of the moment. And it's this flexibility—using the street differently in different situations for different purposes—that provides the opportunity to create a variety of different experiences.

For example, back in 2008, Main Street was shut down for the premiere of *Swing Vote*, a movie starring Kevin Costner, complete with a red carpet running across the street. Later Costner's band played a concert on a stage set up on downtown's 100 percent corner, Main and California Streets, with the California Street hill leading up to the city hall serving as a natural amphitheater. (Costner counts Ventura as his hometown and returned to Main Street a decade later to participate in a benefit concert for victims of the Thomas Fire, which burned for more than a month beginning in December 2017.)

But the Costner concert wasn't an aberration. Several times a year, Main Street gets shut down for parades and street fairs, which is part of the reason Main Street Moves was implemented without much resistance. There's something about closing a downtown street to traffic that's magical. Downtowns are usually dense places, with buildings close to the street. This urban structure crowds people closer together, whether they are watching a parade, dancing at a concert, or strolling among booths at a street fair. Closing a wide suburban street to traffic just isn't the same.

Of course, closing a street to traffic also allows you to introduce a bit of whimsy that isn't usually possible when cars are whizzing by. Consider the story of Sham Hock, a giant inflatable green pig whose life and tragic demise are inextricably linked to Ventura's Main Street. For many years, Hock had been one of the highlights of the city's annual St. Patrick's Day parade along Main Street, his inflated smile beaming at everyone along the parade route. During the 2017 parade, to the dismay of his fans, Hock deflated in front of the judging table on Main Street, right near the library. A few months later, Ventura's civic leaders led a funeral parade down Main Street to honor him.

But a great street doesn't have to be closed to traffic to be great, as long as it's designed for people as well as cars. Main Street in downtown Ventura is wide, but there's diagonal parking, so there's only one driving lane in each direction. The locals know to drive slow. In most places, the sidewalk is actually wider than the driving lane—about twice as wide as the typical sidewalk. You can walk hand-in-hand and people coming the other way can still pass you. Unlike most streets in U.S. cities, Main Street is designed so that you feel like you belong there if you're walking.

Partly for this reason, Main Street has always felt almost as if it's part of my house—my front hallway, connecting me to the world. This was especially true in the years I lived in the big blue Victorian—but I also felt it during the fourteen years I had an office downtown and lived elsewhere in Ventura. I would often go three or four days during the week without getting into my car, while I used Main Street as a lifeline to everything I needed. Restaurants, stores, the city hall, the library, the bank, my office—all were within three or four blocks of where I lived, and most were along Main Street. Especially during the years when I was in politics, I'd often bump into people I needed to talk to at some point along Main Street—everyone from the city manager and prominent business owners down to ordinary folks who would stop me and give me hell, which I sometimes deserved.

We usually think of this kind of lifestyle as something only available to people who live in large cities. After all, most of us live most of our lives buckled into cars, driving around auto-bound suburbs. But a great street like Main Street in Ventura can create this experience in a city of any size.

I found that the small-town urbanism Main Street brings to Ventura made me a better parent, especially after I got divorced when my daughter was an adolescent.

In *A Better Place to Live*, Philip Langdon recalls that growing up in a small but walkable town in Upstate New York in the 1950s, he didn't have the typical American experience of being chauffeured around until he was sixteen and then suddenly being thrown the car keys. Rather, because he could walk and bike on his own from a young age, he was able to expand his world little by little, exploring farther and farther away from home as he got older—a much richer and healthier childhood experience.

Because Main Street is a great street, my daughter—growing up in at the start of the twenty-first century—was able to have the same kind of experience as Langdon. From adolescence, she walked to stores to buy gifts for her friends, Starbucks to drink coffee and people-watch, the movie theater with her friends, the park to play with her dog, and even her mother's office—all of which were within walking distance on Main Street.

She often felt cooped up in the Victorian, which didn't have a yard. She begged me to let her jog, even after dark. Finally I agreed to let her go jogging, but only if she stayed on Main Street between the house and Mission San Buenaventura—knowing that two beloved Main Street business owners, Clary Rudd of Bank of Books and Chang Liampetchakul of Tipps Thai, were always watching the street. They'd see her go in one direction and look out to make sure she came back.

In part, I suppose, that's just small-town America. But my daughter wouldn't have had the same experience even in a small-town suburb. The qualities that make Main Street a great street played a critical role in her growing up into the person she is today.

Main Street actually does go somewhere. All in all it is six miles long, connecting Highway 101 just west of downtown to another section of Highway 101 in East Ventura. Along its course it flows through all different kinds of neighborhoods—not just downtown Ventura but the prewar commercial strip of midtown, alongside Ventura High School, the city's pioneer cemetery, and Community Memorial Hospital; past Pacific View Mall; underneath a different freeway (Highway 126); and finally through a congested suburban shopping zone that includes Target, among other stores. Down that way it serves as a street that exclusively moves cars, although because of the congestion, they don't go very fast on that stretch of Main Street either.

But that doesn't take anything away from the qualities that make it my favorite street. I don't know whether Main Street Moves will be permanent, although it will continue to flex between being open and closed to cars depending on the situation. In that regard, I think Ventura can use Main Street to lead the way in the post-pandemic world, where our built environment must be flexible and adaptable rather than rigid. In a world flooded with SUVs and pickup trucks, that's quite an accomplishment.

PART 2

PROSPERITY

Perhaps because I am from a small, long-declining factory town, I have always been keenly attuned to the relationship between place and prosperity. As I wrote in the introduction to this book, I spent much of my childhood exploring old industrial and commercial facilities, fascinated by what they told me about both place and prosperity.

We don't always consciously connect place and prosperity; economists tend to think of economic activity as an abstract concept separated from any particular location. But of course all economic activity occurs in the context of a place, and it will not occur at all if the place does not facilitate it with infrastructure, access to a labor force, and a local supply chain. Simply put, prosperity requires a good place, and prosperous cities are usually good places.

One great challenge to placemakers today is to ensure that the prosperity that creates great places is widely shared. As I note in the final essay in this section, I fear that at a time of great income inequality, it may simply be beyond the capability of a city or a place to ensure that everyone benefits from prosperity. But it is surely true that we cannot have widespread prosperity without investing in good places in all neighborhoods and communities, not just some.

CHAPTER 10
Romancing the Smokestack

Back in the '80s, when I first started writing about economic development, the governors of seven states went on *The Phil Donahue Show*, the premiere daytime talk show of its time and begged General Motors to build the assembly plant for its brand-new Saturn brand in their states. It was, to put it bluntly, a pathetic excuse for an economic development campaign. Even though auto assembly plants don't literally have smokestacks, this was a stark example of politicians trying to find a shortcut to economic success through the standard technique of "romancing the smokestack"—wooing some out-of-town business in hopes that it will come to town. I always counted the *Donahue Show* as the lowest point in the history of American economic development, especially since none of the seven states got the plant.

At least the *Donahue Show* seemed like the low point—until 2010, when Ohio Governor Ted Strickland made a YouTube music video begging basketball star LeBron James to re-sign with the Cleveland Cavaliers. The music video was even more of a low point than the *Donahue* episode because it managed to trivialize both the economic development goal and the means by which that goal is pursued. Somehow a talk show seems almost statesmanlike compared to a music video. And have we sunk so low that the holy grail of economic development is not an auto assembly plant, but an individual basketball player? Not that it much mattered. In the end, making a music video didn't work any better than going on a talk show. The Saturn plant went to Tennessee—at least until GM killed the brand in 2009—and LeBron went to Miami (before he came back to Cleveland and eventually went to Los Angeles).

If the humorous failures listed above teach us anything, it is this: There is no magic bullet for prosperity. You can't just romance the smokestack and hope to succeed, especially in the long run. But there are ways to maximize the chance of enduring success.

The fact that some communities are prosperous and some are not is hardly an accident. In large part, success is the result of deliberate effort on the part of business organizations, nonprofit entities such as research institutions and universities, and—yes—government agencies to nurture the growth and sustainability of particular businesses and particular types of economic growth in particular locations.

There's nothing new about this. For thousands of years, cities and regions have prospered when they have grabbed emerging economic opportunities and found ways to make sure the economic benefit flows toward them. Sometimes these efforts have been mostly private—as when the Columbian Rope Company, in the midst of the Great Depression, set up a research lab in my hometown and hired my grandfather, a chemistry professor, to run it. Sometimes these efforts have been mostly public—as when the Erie Canal was built by New York State and the interstate highway system was financed by the federal government. And sometimes these efforts have been a combination—as when Congress subsidized the private construction of the transcontinental railroad.

But in the last couple of decades, the activist role of local and regional players has become more evident. Silicon Valley is part of a worldwide economic elite largely because of the presence of Stanford University and the way entrepreneurs have leveraged Stanford's presence. Dallas and Denver are major cities largely because civic and political leaders built enormous airports—what one former Dallas mayor called "the port to the ocean of the air"—at a time when nobody else was doing so. Pittsburgh continues to prosper—despite the departure of its steel mills and a steady decline in population—because it has reinvented its economy over and over again, using the intellectual capital housed at Carnegie Mellon University.

These places are prosperous specifically because they have *not* tried to romance the smokestack into town. They know that prosperity isn't dependent on one company or one plant or one person. Prosperity—especially the kind that endures for decades—emerges from a carefully constructed ecosystem that nurtures and sustains skilled labor, innovative entrepreneurs, research breakthroughs, and well-capitalized start-ups. Such an ecosystem builds on the strengths that already exist in a city, a region, or a state, and as it spins off wealth, it plows a good portion of the profit back into the enterprise.

As the stories about the Saturn plant and LeBron James—and more recent stories like Amazon's unsuccessful foray into Queens—suggest, this kind of nurturing of the ecosystem is not always the popular image of economic development. Economic developers are sometimes viewed as the public-sector equivalent of corporate raiders, going around and stealing businesses from one another at the public's expense. At its worst, economic development really is no better than that. But at its best, economic development is a miraculous thing to behold, as cities and states and universities and business organizations work together to take advantage of emerging opportunities and create enduring prosperity for a community and its people.

Much of my writing about economic development, going back to the late 1980s, has been for *Governing* magazine. For a while, the joke at *Governing* was that I was the "panacea editor," since my job was mostly to write lengthy articles about the latest economic development fad—auto assembly plants, convention centers, ballparks, entertainment-oriented downtowns—and prove that whatever I was writing about was not a panacea. But I have also enjoyed highlighting things I saw in my travels (nothing was ever more fun than the middle-of-the-night tour of the Federal Express operation in Memphis) and, often, things that were just plain counterintuitive (like the idea that China is losing manufacturing jobs just like we are).

Of course, my perspective has changed dramatically during this time. When I wrote my first economic development column for *Governing*, I was a journalist and teacher, and my daughter was in kindergarten. I had spent most of my life observing and commenting, often at the thirty-thousand-foot level. When I wrote "Romancing the Smokestack," I was a professional planning consultant and had just been sworn in as mayor of my city, and my daughter was in college. In contrast to previous phases of my career, I spent every minute of every day trying to make things happen on the ground. Obviously, I had a different perspective as a mayor and practitioner than as journalist—less idealistic and less focused on sweeping trends; more pragmatic and more focused on the nuts and bolts of the everyday business of economic development.

Through it all, however, I have never ceased to be fascinated by the process of how cities, regions, and states build prosperity and then how they maintain it over the long term. Great cities, large and small, are powered by great prosperity, and the smartest cities—just like the smartest businesses—understand that they have to continuously plow the fruits of their prosperity into sustaining and reinventing themselves. It's a mysterious process, but it's pretty miraculous when it works.

CHAPTER 11

Company Town

For years, I have played this parlor game with my family that drives them crazy. They have all heard me say a million times that all movies are about urban planning, so they always try to get me to tell him how this or that movie is really about urban planning.

So we emerge from, say, *Lord of the Rings: Return of the King*, and my daughter says, "Okay, Dad, how was that one about urban planning?" In response, I am incredulous. "It's obvious," I say—that's how I always begin my answer—"It's obvious that it's about competing paradigms about how to create urban places. Remember that capital city up on the steep hill? That's the classic medieval city. Go read your Lewis Mumford—don't you get it?"

But when I say that all movies are about urban planning, I really mean all filmed entertainment is really rooted in the concept of place. And the place depicted is always a character in the movie or television show even if it's not visually present. You can't think of Mary Tyler Moore—if you're old enough to remember her—without thinking of Minneapolis. You can't think of *Seinfeld* or *Friends* without thinking of Manhattan. You can't think of *Chinatown* without thinking of Los

Angeles or *Driving Miss Daisy* without thinking of Atlanta. Because one of the most compelling parts of filmed entertainment is that it is so good at fabricating place.

Inevitably, the location of a movie or television show becomes a part of the experience and part of the emotional appeal. Even when the place fabricated is not in Los Angeles it becomes a tourist attraction. In the 1980s, one of the most popular shows on television, the sitcom *Cheers*, was filmed in Los Angeles about a bar that didn't exist in Boston. Twenty years later, the bar in Boston that didn't exist where they never filmed the show was a tourist attraction.

Of course, if you live in Los Angeles, this whole set of connections gets even more complicated. When you think of Mary Tyler Moore, you think not only of Minneapolis, but of CBS Television City in Los Angeles at Beverly and Fairfax, right near Farmers Market and The Grove, where *The Mary Tyler Moore Show* was filmed. And then there's the way in which everyone in the world knows Los Angeles visually even though they've never been there. When I moved there at age twenty-five—having never been on the West Coast before—I was amazed at how much of it I knew and understood just from watching TV thousands of miles away in Upstate New York as a kid. (After living in Southern California for decades, I'm now on the opposite side of that one. I can't just watch a car chase on a typical cop show—I have to squint to see the background so I can search for familiar restaurants, familiar stores, and even familiar parking spaces.)

As an urban planner, I have always made the mistake of thinking of "Hollywood" almost exclusively as a physical place. The first scholarly article I ever wrote was actually about the development of Hollywood up until 1910—before the movies. But to think of Hollywood exclusively as a real place, of course, is to miss the point.

In 1987, on the occasion of the seventy-fifth anniversary of Paramount Pictures, I got an assignment to interview Frank Mancuso, then head of Paramount. Then a modestly paid freelance journalist, I drove up to the famous front gate of Paramount in my green 1977 Honda Civic (which had a nail sticking out of the steering wheel where I had attempted to replace a screw) and I said to the security guard, "I'm here to see Frank Mancuso, the head of the studio!" The guard checked his sheet about three times and asked to see my driver's license before finally waving me through.

One interesting thing about Mancuso was that he had grown up on the distribution and exhibition side of the business, not the production side. The production people live in Los Angeles, but the distribution and exhibition people are scattered all over the United States. He had never lived in Los Angeles before he came in as head of Paramount. For a while, he was even stationed in Buffalo. I wanted to ask him about this, so I brought it up with the Paramount public relations person while I was waiting to see him.

I made the mistake of phrasing my question like this: "Do you think Mr. Mancuso's view of the industry is different because he has not worked in Hollywood for most of his career?"

If I hadn't looked like a greenhorn in my '77 Honda Civic, I sure looked like one now. She simply didn't understand the question. In her mind, Mancuso had worked in Hollywood his whole career. Because he had spent his whole career working in the movie business—and wherever the movie business exists, that's Hollywood. I had made the mistake of confusing the real Hollywood with the imaginary one, and even people who work for the studios don't do that.

The intersection of Hollywood's fabricated geography and Los Angeles's real-world geography has produced one of the great economic development stories in the history of the United States. Between 1880 and 1910, real estate and civic leaders—operating for their own venal purposes but also out of a sense of destiny—laid the foundation for a great metropolis of some kind. Ruthlessly and relentlessly, they imported water, houses, and people, and they waited for something to happen. And within a few years, the perfect industry came along—one that was very young, growing fast, glamorous, and exploited Los Angeles's assets perfectly.

What happened was typical of how manufacturing businesses locate and exploit factory towns. Los Angeles had the raw material, which was climate, but also a young and bustling city that could serve as a backdrop. LA had land, which was cheap, and isolation, which is sometimes necessary in company towns. And LA quickly developed the labor pool needed to fabricate. So the fledging studios gradually created campuses and walled them off and the ordinary folks who worked in the studios lived in the bungalow neighborhoods that were built nearby. In other words, the studios were factories and the bungalow streets were factory-gate neighborhoods. Los Angeles was a factory town.

A century later Los Angeles is not a Rust Belt town—at least not insofar as the entertainment industry is concerned—but the world is different. All the qualities listed earlier—climate, isolation, cheap land, labor—have either gone away or are not viewed so much as assets anymore. Los Angeles is expensive, it's landlocked, and it's no longer isolated. There's this constant fear that it's going to lose "The Industry," and everybody in town is hard-pressed for a solution. Will we lose the industry? Do we have to subsidize movie moguls to keep it?

When I first began writing about this question as a magazine journalist in the late 1980s and early 1990s, this was a very big fear because production—by which I mean actual shooting, both on location and in soundstages—was drifting away. It was going to Vancouver and to Toronto, and for a while it seemed like it was going everywhere. Throughout the country, cities and states appeared willing to do anything to meet the almost impossible demands of the entertainment industry, whose functionaries are as likely as not to call some state bureaucrat in the middle of the night asking for "a forty-year-old Caucasian female with three fingers missing off her left hand." When this very request came into one state's film office from *Alfred Hitchcock Presents*, the state's film liaison called the Governor's Commission on the Handicapped, which came up with three such Caucasian females willing to make their hands available for filming at no charge. In Los Angeles, by contrast, even the rates charged for such a role seem more like extortion than fees.

In particular, Los Angeles seemed vulnerable at that time to what I called the New York–Orlando axis. Orlando was cheap and had a lot of land and a warm climate—kind of like Los Angeles in 1910. Led by Disney, all the studios were setting up shop there. So Orlando had brand-new facilities—and could import actors from New York for the day because it's in the same time zone and it's only about a two-and-a-half-hour flight. You could fly from New York to Orlando, do a television commercial, and fly back on the same day. The way things were going, it seemed that Los Angeles's role would soon be reduced to providing expensive restaurants where moguls and producers could have lunch.

When I lived in Los Angeles, there was a newspaper article slamming Governor Arnold Schwarzenegger, of all people, for not paying enough attention to the entertainment industry's problems. And there is always the possibility of an unexpected collapse. I point this out because I grew up in New York State in the 1960s and 1970s. A collapse was inconceivable in New York in 1960. But New York's economy *did* collapse in the 1970s. Just because it's inconceivable in Los Angeles today doesn't mean it can't happen.

By and large, however, the industry has stayed there. To my mind, there are three critical factors that together suggest that even now Los Angeles has the ability to hang onto the entertainment industry and use it to shape the area's economy and urban geography well into the future. Indeed, many of today's trends in the entertainment industry conform nicely today to the emerging patterns and trends in economic development throughout the world.

First, Los Angeles still has an entertainment industry infrastructure unparalleled anywhere in the world. Most experts tend to focus on the labor pool, which is extremely important, but when I tend to focus on what you might call "stuff." Los Angeles has more entertainment industry "stuff" than anywhere else.

For me, exhibit number one was my father-in-law's prop rental house, which specialized in antiques and was located on Gower Street, around the corner from Paramount, for more than sixty years. Watching this business operate made me realize that the entertainment industry operates under its own rules that, while they might seem odd, are actually very logical and mostly favor Los Angeles.

Let's say, for example, that some studio wants to film an antebellum melodrama. The location scout goes to Mississippi to find just the right plantation to rent for the shooting. Meanwhile, however, the set decorator goes to the prop house on Gower and picks out all the antiques that will be used on the set. A tractor-trailer then backs up to the prop house, where the antiques are loaded and shipped to Mississippi. They sit in the mansion during location shooting for three months, and then they're shipped back to Gower Street, where they might be rented out a week later for some television pilot.

This might seem like an odd way to run an industry, but there actually is an economic efficiency to it. Like hundreds or even thousands of other items required to make movies and television shows, these antiques are readily available here in Los Angeles. Everybody knows where they are and how to rent them. It would be very hard to replicate this system anywhere else.

The second critical factor has to do with technology. In looking at the history of the entertainment industry, the only times we've seen a change in the center of gravity geographically has been at a time of technological change. And in each case, this change has resulted in a further shift from New York to Los Angeles.

At the beginning of the twentieth century, there was no such thing as filmed entertainment. All entertainment in the United States was live—and both the talent and infrastructure for the business were based in New York City. This was true not only of Broadway, which provided high-class entertainment in Manhattan and selected other locations, but it was also true of vaudeville, which was essentially an ongoing national tour of live low-brow and middle-brow entertainment.

The first technological shift came when silent movies first became popular—between 1910 and 1920—and quickly began to replace vaudeville as the inexpensive entertainment of choice in towns all over the United States. In that one ten-year period, Los Angeles went from being a real estate scam that most people had never heard of to the worldwide center of a fast-growing and glamorous business that thrived on cutting-edge technology. Hollywood went, quite literally, from a teetotaling community of lemon grovers to a place so rich and famous that semi-precious stones were embedded in the cornices of local bank buildings.

A second technological change that favored Los Angeles was the advent of talkies in the late 1920s. There was nothing inevitable about this innovation at the time. Not all the inventors working on talkies lived in California—indeed, one of them, Theodore Case, invented the "Fox Movietone" method in my hometown of Auburn in Upstate New York—and all the talkers were in New York City, where theater still ruled. At first, talkies led to an uptick in shooting in New York. The first two Marx Brothers movies—*The Cocoanuts* and *Animal Crackers*—were shot in Astoria, Queens, during the daytime while the brothers were working on Broadway at night. Soon enough, however, the talkers and writers moved to Los Angeles and started working on talkies. It wasn't long before they all started writing and talking *about* Hollywood and Los Angeles, for better or worse, in such novels as *The Day of the Locust* by Nathaniel West and *The Last Tycoon* by F. Scott Fitzgerald. The die was cast.

The third technological shift occurred when Baby Boomers like me were children. At first, television, like talkies, seemed to signal a revival in New York, because the TV networks were based there and TV had to be done live, usually with theatrical actors. The advent of filmed television, however, led once again to a significant shift from New York to Los Angeles. In the mid-1950s, when I was born, most television was live and done from New York. By the mid-1960s, when I was a boob-tubing elementary-school student, most TV was filmed and done from Los Angeles. In fact, one of the most popular shows of that period, *The Dick Van Dyke Show*, contained a kind of ironic joke that I didn't get at the time: It was a comedy show filmed in Los Angeles about a comedy show broadcast live from New York. At that point we couldn't let go of the idea that New York was the center of entertainment, even though the entertainment that was about New York being the center of entertainment was created in Los Angeles.

Thanks in part to the pandemic, we are now in the midst of the fourth technological shift—a shift from entertainment delivered mostly in movies theaters and on television to entertainment delivered mostly over the internet. It is hard to know whether this shift, like the previous ones, will favor Los Angeles. It will almost certainly favor California, since the internet companies, like Apple, are mostly based here and have close ties to the LA-based entertainment industry. Production is likely to decentralize even more as the internet drives down costs. But history suggests that Los Angeles will somehow wind up as a winner, though.

The third critical factor that favors Los Angeles's ability to hang onto the entertainment industry has to do with the changing nature of how cities succeed in building prosperity. In the industrial era, prosperity followed the factory model: The key was converting raw materials into manufactured products, which occurred in a closed setting that was proprietary and completely controlled by the company. Your research lab developed new processes, and products were manufactured with a labor pool that basically devoted a lifetime to working at the factory. This was how the factories in my hometown worked, including the rope factory where my grandfather ran the research lab. It was also how the Hollywood studios worked up through the 1940s, when they followed the factory model.

Eventually things changed. It wasn't just that factories closed, although they did. What really happened was that the industrial economy flew apart geographically, with assembly plants landing in one place, research and development operations in another, corporate headquarters in another. To succeed, cities had to shift from the factory-town model— where prosperity assumed a cradle-to-grave economic process all in the same town—to more of an open model, where the cities focused on grabbing and strengthening the pieces of the economic process that they knew they could retain. In the United States, with its high labor costs, this meant focusing on the high-value-added portions of the economic process, such as R&D, rather than on assembling manufacturing goods, which couldn't support high wages anymore.

This new approach placed great emphasis on three things that are now commonly viewed as keys to success in building prosperity today, and they all represent the opposite of the traditional model: institutions, especially educational and medical institutions, that are deeply embedded in a place and unlikely to move, rather than footloose factories; a pool of labor talent that is both highly skilled and free-floating within the metropolitan area and therefore able to be efficiently redeployed when new opportunities come along, rather than unionized employees that represent a heavy fixed cost; and an "open innovation" model in which research and development efforts are usually pursued openly, often in collaboration between business and universities, rather than proprietary research labs. This looks a lot like the entertainment industry in Los Angeles today.

The embedded institutions are not just the studios themselves but, increasingly, as in the case of other economic sectors, the research and educational entities that have been created in the entertainment industry. Instead of Paramount and Universal, the embedded institutions are places like the American Film Institute and the film schools at UCLA and USC. These institutions are well established and well endowed, and they are not going to move. They will continue to draw entertainment industry talent to Los Angeles no matter where the location shooting goes.

As for a highly skilled free-floating labor pool, the entertainment industry converted to a "jobber" industry sooner than almost any other industry in the United States shortly after the studio "factories" disappeared in the 1950s and 1960s. That's one reason the entertainment industry can support high salaries even for craft workers. The industry's labor force can be redeployed rapidly and efficiently, and if there is a slowdown, no large "factory" is carrying the ongoing cost of the labor.

As for open innovation, is there any good script that nobody in town knows about? Scripts are the intellectual capital of the entertainment industry—the product R&D, if you will—and everybody's read everything. Open innovation is a long-standing tradition in Hollywood.

One additional factor—not always on the economic development short list—is the way older industrial cities skillfully reuse their mills and factories for new purposes, often as tourist attractions. And here too Los Angeles is no different. Just as old mills in New England now serve as outlet malls—giving visitors both good bargains and a taste of the industrial era—Hollywood's factories are gradually turning into tourist attractions such as the Universal Studio Tour, reusing an old economic asset while reinforcing in the public's mind the idea that LA is the center of the industry.

Los Angeles's political leaders have long struggled with the question of how to keep the industry and in particular how to keep location shooting and production work there. But this begs a more basic question: Do we really want to? Location shooting is kind of like assembly-line work—it's a relatively small part of the process that does not add a lot of economic value and is extremely sensitive to cost. Using subsidies and other extraordinary measures to keep location shooting in Los Angeles is like using deep subsidies to keep assembly-line jobs from going to China. In the long run it's not going to work. Some shooting and a lot of pre- and postproduction work will continue to take place in LA because this is where the industry is centered, but shooting is not what's most important.

What *is* important is how to support this mature industry that is now operating in a high-cost, landlocked environment. What other pieces of economic infrastructure does this industry need? How should it be provided? Do we need to focus on getting the physical facilities—something that the planning process is often good at delivering? How do we make sure that the labor pool of the next generation, especially in the not-so-glitzy jobs, is being recruited and trained, especially in light of extremely high housing costs and killer traffic congestion?

In the early 1970s, the great architectural historian Reyner Banham called Los Angeles a city that was one hundred miles wide but barely one hundred years deep. Today, Los Angeles is a different city—crowded and expensive and mature—and the entertainment industry is as embedded in this place as any industry is in any place in the world. As we think about the maturation of Los Angeles as an urban place, we have to think about the entertainment industry in a different way. We can't think just how to protect location shooting or find some way to provide more cheap land to the studies. We have to focus on how to build on the labor pool, the infrastructure, the suppliers—the *stuff*, if you will—that will be required to ensure that Los Angeles prospers from the entertainment industry as much in its second century as it did in its first.

CHAPTER 12

The Case for Subsidizing the Mermaid Bar

George Skelton, the venerable *Los Angeles Times* political columnist, came out in favor of Governor Jerry Brown's plan to eliminate redevelopment in 2011. Skelton's exhibit number one was Dive Bar, a hangout on derelict K Street in downtown Sacramento that was one of the city's hottest night spots—complete with a tank over the bar where women dressed as mermaids swam—thanks partly to the redevelopment subsidies provided to the project's developer.

"Look, I've got nothing against mermaid bars," wrote Skelton, who is widely admired for his thoughtful, commonsense viewpoint. "In fact, state government used to work best when legislators hung out in one near the Capitol. I just question whether state government—any government—should be helping to pay for a mermaid bar."

Skelton's comments reminded me of Zev Yaroslavky's rant in the 1990s, back when Yaroslavky was on the Los Angeles City Council, that redevelopment funds should not be used to subsidize theaters and nightspots in downtown Los Angeles "just so yuppies can dance on Spring Street."

I've got more than a little sympathy for this viewpoint. I've been

The mermaid Dive Bar, Sacramento, California *(Credit: Chris Hoene)*

critical of redevelopment over the years, especially the way cities have played the redevelopment game for their own narrow financial gain. And I remain something of critic today. At the time of this debate, I was mayor and, hence, the chair of a city redevelopment commission.

But there's a legitimate public policy argument for subsidizing mermaid bars. It's kind of complicated and has a lot of caveats, which I'll get to at the end. Ultimately, it's about creating compact, compelling places in urban locations—a form of human settlement that is probably more fiscally and environmentally sustainable than sprawl—so that more people will live and work in such locations.

Redevelopment is a mechanism to stimulate and direct real estate development. The point of redevelopment is to direct both public and private investment into specific geographical areas—often older areas that have become run down and are suffering from disinvestment. The original urban renewal–type reasons for this governmental intervention still stand: The more these older areas slide, the more they will cost the government in police protection, social services, and other costs associated with dysfunction.

Of course, there are plenty of places in California that need stimulated investment more than K Street (though it remains a stubbornly derelict street surrounded by renewed urban affluence), and there are plenty of ways to stimulate investment other than subsidizing a bar with women swimming around a mermaid tank above it. But the move toward encouraging compact urban development in California makes the argument for certain types of redevelopment subsidies even more compelling. Infill development is more expensive than greenfield development, so, all other things being equal, it'll be at a disadvantage. But in the long run laying down infrastructure in sprawling greenfield locations is inefficient and more expensive. Furthermore, encouraging people to live and work in compact urban neighborhoods yields an enormous environmental benefit, especially in reducing the overall amount of driving and, consequently, greenhouse gas emissions, overall gasoline usage, and other pollutants.

You might be thinking my argument is that a mermaid bar on K Street is far more cost-effective and environmentally beneficial than a mermaid bar in an auto-oriented strip mall in Roseville. This is partly right, but there's more to it than that. People make choices about where they live, work, and otherwise spend their time not based on proximity to mermaid bars alone, but based on their overall sense of whether the community meets their needs—jobs, amenities, schools, recreation, shopping, and so forth. Any successful developer will tell you that in order to succeed in the marketplace, they either have to provide all these things or make sure they are close by. And what those amenities are will differ depending on the market you're aiming for.

So if public policy efforts are going to be geared toward creating urban communities that are compact and efficient yet also complete communities that are competitive with sprawling alternatives, those policy efforts will include providing people with amenities they want, like shopping centers, golf courses, schools, or even bars. (To be fair, in the case of Dive Bar, the redevelopment agency subsidized a developer who built a project and then found the mermaid bar as a tenant.)

The obvious question that arises is why the market can't provide mermaid bars on its own. After all, our cities are crawling with urban hipsters young and old these days (not the least of whom was Governor Jerry Brown himself, who lived in a redevelopment-subsidized loft a few blocks away from the mermaid bar). Can't a mermaid bar survive on its own without redevelopment subsidies? Or, more to the point, wouldn't hipsters live in urban locations with or without redevelopment subsidies?

That's the eternal question about redevelopment—and it is, in part, unanswerable. The only serious policy research ever done on the question of whether all that tax revenue generated in redevelopment areas would have occurred anyway answered that question with a solid maybe. So I don't have hard numbers to back me up. But my instinct tells me that given the complexity of urban development, a lot of this stuff would never get built without redevelopment subsidies. Our cities would suffer as a result, and we'd have more sprawl and less compact development. For my money, that's bad for everybody.

But I'm willing to admit that cities in California have gotten so used to redevelopment as being their first, last, and only way to do things that they've forgotten that other ways might work just as well. After all, the goal here isn't to figure how to funnel property tax money to developers. The goal is to figure out how to make urban development projects be profitable enough to actually build. Redevelopment may be an effective way of doing that—and it may be the way California cities are used to—but it's not the only way.

In the end, it wasn't the redevelopment subsidies that succeeded in persuading the yuppies—or, to update Yaroslavsky's term, hipsters—to dance on Spring Street in downtown LA. Instead, it was a very simple policy change instituted by Mayor James Hahn in 2001 that waived all parking requirements for adaptive reuse projects downtown and in Hollywood. With the stroke of a pen, Hahn turned the conversion of old office buildings into lofts from a money loser into a desirable real estate investment. Eliminating the parking requirement put money in developers' pockets—or, at least, their pro formas—just as surely as a redevelopment subsidy.

The mermaid bar on K Street in Sacramento is still there, though K Street itself remains stubbornly resistant to gentrification. Long gone is the whole redevelopment process itself, which was eliminated by Governor Jerry Brown to help balance the state budget shortly after George Skelton wrote his piece. But the bottom line is that there's a pretty compelling argument for subsidizing the mermaid bar no matter what Skelton thinks. It is probably necessary to provide government subsidies to infill urban development in order to offset the increased short-term cost of such development compared to greenfield development in the suburbs, whose long-term societal costs are not built into anybody's pro forma.

CHAPTER 13
Kotkin versus Florida

In the Spring 2021 issue of *City Journal,* a savvy publication about urban affairs published by the right-leaning Manhattan Institute, one article stood out: a piece titled "America's Post-Pandemic Geography." It was a wide-ranging tour of how cities in the United States were likely to change after the COVID-19 pandemic. And it was very carefully balanced: Superstar cities would struggle, but they would bounce back. Suburbs would thrive, but the successful ones would become more like cities. Rural communities were growing rapidly—but only some of them that had been growing even before the pandemic.

Almost more important than the contents of the piece, which were somewhat predictable, were the authors: Richard Florida, the upbeat urbanist who became famous because of his book *The Rise of the Creative Class,* and Joel Kotkin, the grumpy defender of the suburbs who has been highly critical of cities in the United States. Florida and Kotkin had been bumping heads for twenty years—and Kotkin, in particular, had attacked Florida's ideas vigorously in the past, often in the pages of *City Journal.*

What a difference a pandemic makes. All through COVID, Florida and Kotkin were on Zoom, constantly talking about their vision for the future of US cities and suburbs. Florida appeared on webinar after webinar from his winter home in Miami Beach, carefully coiffed with designer glasses. (He teaches at the University of Toronto the rest of the year.) Kotkin appeared on his own podcast series from his disheveled home office in Orange County, California. (He's affiliated with the right-leaning Chapman University.) And they tag-teamed a wide variety of Zooms and webinars to talk about cities after COVID.

Their growing partnership apparently grew out of a joint effort with the think tank Heartland Forward to assess the future of northwest Arkansas, funded by the Walton Family Foundation. But it was a surprise nevertheless. And it's hard to say at this point what the newfound Kotkin-Florida partnership will produce in the future—or what it means about the future of cities—because for two decades, no two urbanists have had more divergent views.

In a nutshell, Florida's argument in *The Creative Class* was that to be successful, cities have to be cool. The engine of the US economy, he claimed, was creativity. The United States had produced a "creative class" of close to forty million highly educated professionals who focused on researching and creating innovative products. And catering to these folks—primarily by creating cities they like—was the key to future economic growth for the country. The book was a best seller, and the "creative class" became a widely used term of art in urban planning.

No sooner had Florida declared that cities had to be cool, however, than Kotkin starting writing that cities wouldn't succeed unless they were *un*cool. Kotkin had long been a fan of what he calls "nerdistans"—boring suburbs (he always seems to mention Irvine) that nevertheless house some of the most powerful drivers of the US economy, especially in the tech sectors. But Florida's work really revved Kotkin up. In a typical article in *City Journal* in 2006, Kotkin called the cool cities idea "shtick" and suggested that the creative class "by the time they get into their 30s, may be more interested in economic opportunity, a single family house and procreation than remaining 'hip and cool' urbanites."

The question of how to rebuild New Orleans after Hurricane Katrina in 2005 gave Kotkin a special opportunity to wave the flag for uncool cities. Less than a week after the hurricane, he drew a line in the sand. "The wrong approach would be to preserve a chimera of the past, producing a touristic faux New Orleans, a Cajun Disneyland," he wrote in the *Los Angeles Times*. Rather, the city should follow Houston's model: "Houston has succeeded by sticking to the basics, by focusing on the practical aspects of urbanism rather than the glamorous." He called the creative class approach "the ephemeral city." (Houston and New Orleans have a close relationship; among other things, Houston welcomed two hundred thousand Katrina refugees, one hundred thousand of whom never went back to New Orleans.)

Nobody followed Kotkin's advice. Over time, New Orleans lost population and diversity, but it became perhaps the most popular city in the South for creative class refugees from the Northeast. And Houston—that hugely successful, somewhat slapped-together, and utilitarian city—pursued an innovation-based creative economy as a way out of its traditional dependence on oil and gas, which was seemingly in decline.

Nevertheless, the contrast between Florida and Kotkin is striking, especially considering the similarity in their backgrounds. Both are from working-class, upwardly mobile families in the New York area. Florida often talks about growing up in New Jersey as the child of an Italian factory worker with a seventh-grade education. Kotkin was born into a Jewish family in New York and grew up on Long Island. But their career paths diverged—and that may account for their difference in perspective.

Florida earned his PhD in urban planning from Columbia University and got a job teaching at Carnegie Mellon University in Pittsburgh. In the 1990s, he observed—and participated in—the revival of a rusted-out old steel town that seemed beyond hope when he arrived. In contrast to other Rust Belt cities such as Buffalo, Cleveland, and Detroit, which have had limited success in revitalization, Pittsburgh came back strong as a tech hub—in large part because of the creative class at Carnegie Mellon, where Florida taught.

Kotkin, by contrast, went to college in California and became a journalist in Los Angeles, where he witnessed firsthand the huge demographic change during the 1980s and 1990s and the vibrant immigrant economy that emerged. His writing in those days displayed a rare understanding of the role that day-to-day, unglamorous business and commerce play in the life of cities. He's always been especially good at explaining small business, immigrant businesses, and the hidden sources of capital in the immigrant community—important stuff in Los Angeles that nobody wrote much about before Kotkin began to highlight it. More recently, he has devoted a lot of effort to lamenting that California, like his beloved New York, is no longer the vehicle for upward mobility that it used to be.

Which is part of the reason he has never been sympathetic to Florida's argument. The creative class might drive economic growth, but, he would argue, it doesn't provide a ladder for upward mobility. Over and over again, Kotkin reduced Florida's creative class argument to nothing more than tourism and entertainment—in other words, bread and circuses. Kotkin has repeated it so frequently that even politicians and economic development experts tout the value of tourism and entertainment and claim they are following Florida's philosophy.

Kotkin's small 2006 book, *The City: A Global History,* provides insight—perhaps unintended—about where he's coming from on cities. In the book, he wrote that cities serve three basic functions: religion, safety, and commerce. His view of cities as centers of commerce is nothing new; from time immemorial, cities have served as the geographical focus of commerce in general and trading in particular. Creating a safe zone goes hand-in-hand with commerce. But Kotkin's deepest conviction seems to concern the role of religion in shaping cities. (He has long been active in Jewish circles himself and was for many years a columnist for the *Jewish Journal,* writing about topics that ranged far beyond cities and suburbs.)

The sacred place is so important to Kotkin that he ended his book with it. He decried that New Urbanists, for example, "rarely refer to the need for a powerful moral vision to hold cities together." He ascribed much of Singapore's recent success to neo-Confucianism. And he decried the modern urban environment, "with its emphasis on faddishness, stylistic issues, and the celebration of the individual over the family or stable community."

This last point was clearly a frontal attack on Florida's ideas, with their emphasis on bohemian aspects of urban life, arts and culture, and the presence of a gay community. It's also, in a way, an attack on the idea of the city as a place of diversity.

But there is more to Florida than art galleries and gay bars, no matter what Kotkin said in those days. In identifying the creative class, he's not just talking about artists and actors. Indeed, if that were all he was talking about, he'd have gotten a lot of play on the Westside of Los Angeles and in Greenwich Village but nowhere else. To Florida, the creative class includes architects, software developers, medical researchers, scientists, engineers—anybody and everybody who is involved in the high-value-added process of conducting basic research and converting that research into new products. And Florida's argument is not that art galleries and gay bars by themselves are economic bonanzas, but that a wide variety of urban amenities are required to attract and retain the key members of the creative class to specific locations.

By and large, Florida is right about what the creative class wants. A while ago I was giving a speech in just about the most blue-collar city you can imagine—Buffalo—and I made the Florida argument. New York State was investing hundreds of millions of dollars in life sciences research in Buffalo in an effort to compete with Georgia, Arizona, and California in this sector of huge economic opportunity. But I pointed out that the prevalent new development pattern in Buffalo was the creation of three-acre suburban lots. I suggested that research scientists trying to cure cancer did not want to spend all weekend on a riding mower.

Afterward, a woman came up to me and told me—in the broadest, flat-a Upstate accent you can imagine—that she worked at a cancer research institute. "You're right," she said of the scientists. "At the end of the day all they want is a restaurant, a gym, and a loft."

It's worth noting that some businesses associated with the ephemeral city actually do represent enormous economic sectors. As Florida protégé Elizabeth Currid-Halkett pointed out in her book about New York City, *The Warhol Economy*, art galleries aren't a very big business, but the fashion industry is a huge industry of worldwide significance. You'd think Kotkin would acknowledge this every once in a while, considering how many times he's told the story, in speeches, about the Lower East Side and the economic miracle of the needle trade in the early 1900s. And in Kotkin's own adopted hometown of Los Angeles, the biggest industry, entertainment, is the most ephemeral of all, with its long history of providing well-paying middle-class craft jobs that have provided a path for upward mobility for generations of families who have lived in Kotkin's own neighborhood.

To his credit, Florida eventually did a mea culpa. In his book *The New Urban Crisis*, published in 2017, he attacked the issue of inequality in cities. He acknowledged that creative class economic development strategies, many of which were derived from his own work, were deepening in inequality problem and limiting the opportunities for upward mobility in just the manner Kotkin suggested.

Kotkin, by contrast, did not do an about-face. In his book *The Human City: Urbanism for the Rest of Us*, also published in 2017, he stuck to his guns in arguing that throughout the world, sprawling, unregulated cities—the kind, he claims, that the creative class doesn't like—provide more economic opportunity, especially for families interested in climbing the ladder into the middle class.

These differences did not stop Florida and Kotkin from working together after their 2017 books were published. They were apparently brought together by Ross DeVol, a respected, right-leaning urban economist who had done a lot of work with Kotkin while at the California-based Milken Institute. DeVol left Milken to start Heartland Forward, an Arkansas-based think tank focused on regional economic development in the middle of the United States, with the support of the Walton Family Foundation. (DeVol's office in Bentonville is around the corner from Sam Walton's original five-and-dime). He brought Kotkin and Florida in as senior fellows, and they worked together on the Northwest Arkansas Economic Recovery Strategy, which was published in October 2020, during the COVID-19 pandemic. The report contained both classic Florida and classic Kotkin strategies—suggesting that Bentonville become the American heartland's center of arts and culture, but *also* a leading center for small business innovation.

Since then, Heartland has followed up with additional studies and reports that Kotkin and Florida have worked on separately rather than together. Nevertheless, the subsequent *City Journal* article, published in the Spring 2021 issue, suggested a rare rapprochement between the leaders of these two competing camps of urbanism.

There's no question that COVID has changed the landscape for urban success in the United States in the twenty-first century; large superstar cities with a big creative class may indeed struggle for a while, and smaller regions—such as Bentonville—have a new shot at success. But if cities large and small do succeed after COVID, they'll do it because they are both cool and uncool.

Kotkin's bottom line remains important: being cool alone will not make US cities work in the twenty-first century. But neither will being uncool. Successful economic development in the twenty-first century will still require that US cities understand the creative class and how to attract and retain those sectors just as Florida suggests. Restoring cities as ladders of upward mobility is a huge challenge, as Kotkin consistently argues, but it's not a goal that is at odds with encouraging the creative class. The high-value-added economy of innovation and creativity remains the underpinning of economic growth in the United States. This economy is based in cities, large and small, and the United States will rise and fall with how successful we are in nurturing this economy in superstar big cities, superstar smaller cities like Bentonville, and suburbs that are becoming more like cities every day.

CHAPTER 14

Houston, We Have a Gentrification Problem

The Sears building in midtown Houston was an iconic retail building if ever there was one. The building was a massive art deco masterpiece designed by a Chicago architectural firm to have no windows (so patrons could focus on shopping, just as casinos allow gamblers to focus on their games) and lots of murals depicting the history of Texas and the future of Houston. Everybody over a certain age in Houston remembers going there to buy their first suit of clothes or Easter dress or their first refrigerator or washing machine.

But nobody who's been around Houston for a long time recognizes the Sears building anymore. After a $100 million investment by Rice University—which owns the property—the store has undergone an enormous transformation into a sun-splashed, wide-open innovation center known as The Ion. Its center atrium doubles as an amphitheater, and the building now features several restaurants, including one that grew out of a nearby food truck. Microsoft and Chevron Technology Ventures are anchor tenants, but there's space for startups as well. The Ion is expected to be the anchor of a sixteen-acre innovation district in rapidly revitalizing midtown Houston, revolving around land owned

The Ion innovation center, Houston, Texas *(Credit: Rice University)*

by Rice, one of the leading science and technology universities in the United States.

The Ion is also on the edge of the Third Ward, a proud African American neighborhood that has, in recent years, experienced rampant land speculation and growing fears of gentrification. So even as it was transforming the Sears building in 2020 and 2021—and laying plans to transform the surrounding neighborhood—Rice was under tremendous pressure to prove that The Ion would benefit everybody in the neighborhood, not just a few technologists. Even some of Rice's own students were leaning on the university to do something big about equity with The Ion.

In response, Rice put together a working group of community leaders, and in the spring of 2021 this group announced its support of what appeared to be a breakthrough "community benefits agreement": a commitment by the university to spending several million dollars in the

Housing in the Third Ward, Houston, Texas
(Credit: Gary Coronado/Copyright Houston Chronicle)

innovation district on things like affordable housing, workforce development, and small business entrepreneurship.

Within hours, however, a group of Third Ward activists slammed the proposed agreement—and, by extension, the entire Ion project—by saying that Rice had "at every step of the Innovation District's development either ignored, directly lied to or subverted the words and aims of residents in the Greater Third Ward area and across the city of Houston." Whether or not the activists' accusations were true, the move was straight out of community organizer Saul Alinsky's *Rules for Radicals* playbook—designed to pressure both Rice and Houston's African American mayor, Sylvester Turner, into providing the neighborhood with even greater concessions.

In decades past, The Ion innovation center would probably have been viewed as an unalloyed victory for Houston. Today, however, this kind of project stimulates a much more nuanced debate over who wins and who loses.

Indeed, in many ways, The Ion battle was similar to a much more widely publicized fight in Queens—the largest borough in New York City in terms of geographical size—over Amazon's proposed second headquarters. In 2017, the e-commerce behemoth set off a classic economic development bidding war by initiating up a competition for a major headquarters-type facility with fifty thousand employees to complement its base in Seattle. Most large cities in the United States entered the competition and ponied up lots of economic development incentives to lure the company. New York City—which was trying to develop a tech hub in West Queens—was one of two winners, offering up a site in Long Island City, just across the East River from Manhattan, and an incentive package worth $1.2 billion. (The commitment of Rice and the City of Houston to The Ion emerged in part from *losing* the Amazon competition.)

Before long, however, lefty progressives in New York—among them Representative Alexandria Ocasio-Cortez, who represents parts of Queens and the Bronx in Congress—pushed back against the deal, in part because of gentrification, saying that housing prices were already going up in Queens in anticipation of Amazon's arrival. They also objected to the city's incentive package. In early 2019, Amazon pulled out of the New York deal, retreating instead to its other winning location—Crystal City in northern Virginia, near the Pentagon.

In other words, it's no longer enough for major economic development efforts to simply stimulate economic growth in a city and revitalize a neighborhood. In an era when income inequality is growing quickly and gentrification fears are rampant, it's possible to revitalize a neighborhood *too much*.

When I first started writing about economic development, the Northeast and the Midwest were first struggling with major factory closings and the deindustrialization of their regional economies. It was a grim time when heavy economic development incentives first became popular as a way to keep factory jobs from leaving and bring new jobs in. Even then, however, there was a counternarrative: Factory jobs will constantly move around the world in search of the cheapest labor, and providing deep subsidies to keep them is a losing battle.

I well remember an economic development expert in Massachusetts saying in the mid-1980s, "If South Carolina wants our factories, go ahead and take them. They'll be gone to Mexico in ten years." The goal shouldn't be to keep any job at all costs, the thinking went, but to retain the high-value-added portions of the product development process in the United States. The low-value-added task of assembling the final products—a portion of the process that had previously provided high-paying unionized jobs for many people with minimal education—simply wasn't worth keeping.

In popular culture, perhaps the best explanation of this view came from John Travolta, playing the Bill Clinton role in *Primary Colors*, telling shipyard workers in New Hampshire, "No politician can reopen this factory, or bring back the shipyard jobs, or make your union strong again. No politician can make it be the way it used to be.... Muscle jobs go where muscle is cheap and that is not here. So if you wanna compete, you're gonna have to exercise a different set of muscles—the ones between your ears."

This was the assumption in the Clinton years: That the United States could prosper by capturing the knowledge-based, high-value-added parts of the manufacturing process—research and development, for example—and let the low-wage parts of manufacturing chase the cheapest workers around the globe. That's the thinking that led to the North American Free Trade Agreement (NAFTA) in the 1990s, which made it much easier to move production out of the United States and then import finished products back.

Of course, the tech revolution began at about the same time—starting with the short-lived internet boom at the turn of the twenty-first century—and that made it possible for economic development experts to envision an entirely different type of US economy than the manufacturing-based economy depended on in the past. From that starting point, it was not much of a leap to Richard Florida's idea that this new economy should depend on the "creative class"—an idea that caused his book to be a best seller in 2002. If the future of the US economy depended on knowledge workers—and, in particular, on the innovation sector driven by the tech revolution—it made sense to focus on the creatives of all types who were driving that economic growth. Thus the focus of economic development shifted from chasing smokestacks to chasing smart kids sitting in coffee shops wearing hoodies and working on their laptops. In the end, the idea was that everybody would benefit from this transition to a knowledge-based, high-value-added economy.

From the beginning, of course, some were skeptical that this shift would work out. After all, most Americans don't have a college degree, and they don't live in the expensive big cities where most of the innovation breakthroughs were taking place. Ross Perot, the irascible third-party presidential candidate in 1992, made a big splash the following year by predicting in a debate with Vice President Al Gore that NAFTA would lead to a "giant sucking sound" as the US manufacturing economy moved to Mexico. He was ridiculed at the time, but as it turned out he was right. The overall manufacturing output of the United States went up, but that was mostly due to automation. The jobs went to Mexico and China.

But then, Richard Florida was right too. Economic growth in the United States *was* driven by urban creatives deeply immersed in the innovation economy, especially in the tech sector. The economic development success stories of the early 2000s weren't the factories or the shopping centers or the convention centers subsidized by government incentives, but the innovation districts—Kendall Square in Cambridge, Mission Bay in San Francisco—that incubated advancements in the technology industry, often in partnership with large research universities. In terms of sheer economic growth, these innovation districts were well worth the effort and investment that cities and universities were putting into them, and on some level there was broad economic benefit. In the early 2010s, Berkeley economist Enrico Moretti pointed out that even service workers in Silicon Valley make significantly higher wages than their counterparts elsewhere.

But fourteen bucks an hour as a barista doesn't help much when the average house goes for a couple million dollars—and therein lay the problem. The tech economy concentrated wealth in a few major cities—New York, San Francisco, Los Angeles—while the rest of the United States was left behind. Even within those cities, some neighborhoods became unbelievably prosperous, while others—only a few miles away or sometimes even a few blocks away—withered. And sometimes, strangely enough, both happened in the same location: A booming tech economy was laid on top of an existing struggling neighborhood.

Previously, the main philosophical battle in economic development in the United States was over subsidies—essentially, who pays. Now the battle was over who reaps the benefits.

And so the globalists got attacked from both the right and the left. The criticism from the right came from advocates of the White working class who eventually became part of the Trump Republican base. The criticism from the left came from progressives—from Alexandria Ocasio-Cortez on down—who believed that a focus on the creative class was leading to and indeed subsidizing gentrification of previously struggling urban neighborhoods.

In response, the right actually embraced traditional smokestack chasing—historically viewed by Republicans as an expensive and inefficient government subsidy—as a way of trying to retain blue-collar manufacturing jobs. Remember Donald Trump's personal intervention, shortly after his election, to save jobs at a Carrier furnace plant in Indianapolis?

In the end, the deal was pretty much just as retro as Trump himself: It depended not so much on the president-elect's intervention as it did on the state of Indiana's $7 million in tax credits. In the end, fewer jobs were saved than Trump promised and lots more went to Mexico. But that didn't diminish the popularity of the idea among the White working class.

The fight on the left over urban gentrification has been much tougher in comparison. Yes, there still were thriving blue-collar economies in the United States—at least in places where the facilities providing those blue-collar jobs could not be moved. One of those places, ironically, was the Houston Ship Channel, the world's largest concentration of petroleum refineries and petrochemical plants, located only a fifteen-minute drive from The Ion. But getting people from places like the Third Ward to places like the Ship Channel was a tough trick—not just geographically, because Houston requires a car to go pretty much anywhere, but perhaps more importantly in terms of skills, because preparing kids growing up in underserved neighborhoods for good-paying blue-collar jobs has proven too difficult for the educational system to achieve.

Which is why, perhaps, left-leaning urban activists focused on gentrification. The Clinton-era idea about high-value-added jobs and knowledge workers hadn't helped everybody. The millennials in the hoodies and laptops sitting in coffee shops were generating enormous economic growth. But the iPhones were being manufactured in China, not Detroit or the east side of Houston.

Because it was occurring literally in the backyards of people who were poor and powerless, gentrification was an obvious target for urban activists. The concept of gentrification has been around since the 1960s. It's a way of describing the process by which affluent folks, mostly White, rediscover long-neglected urban neighborhoods and move in, creating a new kind of urban gentry. Though there's an argument in urban planning that you'd always rather live in a neighborhood that's going up as opposed to one that is going down, there were considerable downsides to gentrification—most notably displacement of longtime residents.

With the new residents often come high property taxes, not very many children, lots of dog walking, and $15 avocado toast. Longtime renters are often squeezed out as rents go up; longtime homeowners often struggle to pay property taxes, though in some cases they can cash in on higher property values. Sometimes homeowners are subject to high-pressure tactics from developers to sell, and renters are encouraged by landlords to move even if they don't want to. At the very least, the culture of the neighborhood changes in a way that doesn't always set well with the longtime residents.

The most famous gentrified neighborhoods were in the Bay Area and New York, specifically Oakland and Brooklyn, those twin urban suburbs that saw the White population grow rapidly because of gentrification after decades of increasing demographic diversification. Gentrification in these two places became a kind of running national joke. *The Onion*, the satirical website, ran a fake story about a tech worker texting his friends as he walked down the street looking at houses in Oakland, causing the prices in the neighborhood to go up $100,000 during his stroll.

But gentrification was a very real issue in virtually every large city, even those between the coasts. Houston gentrified faster than any city in Texas except for Austin, and the Third Ward sat right in the middle of the trend: Located halfway between the two biggest job centers in the region, downtown Houston and the Texas Medical Center; bounded on three sides by affluent neighborhoods; adjacent to the city's only busy light-rail line; and now dealing with The Ion, the emerging symbol of Houston's attempts to create a tech economy that residents feared they would not be part of. No wonder Houston's Third Ward activists turned to tried-and-true community organizing tactics to put pressure on Rice and the city.

In the era of gentrification, however, community organizing had moved past traditional Alinsky *Rules for Radicals*-style methods of bringing outside pressure to bear on the power structure in hopes of getting something—anything—in return. Specifically, in a movement that had begun in Los Angeles, organizers had begun to combat gentrification by using something called a "community benefits agreement"—a series of commitments by a real estate developer, a public agency, or an institution such as Rice meant to ensure that the surrounding neighborhood benefited from the project in question. In one of the largest community benefits agreements ever negotiated, Los Angeles International Airport (LAX) committed to a vast range of obligations, including a living wage policy, job training, and employment preference for low-income residents living near the airport, as well a host of environmental mitigations ranging from electrification of gates to cargo operations and hangers. LAX even committed to conduct a series of studies on health impacts and environmental justice. The agreement was executed between LAX and a coalition of labor, environmental, and community groups—and progress was being tracked by an independent organization charged with monitoring the situation.

At The Ion, Rice made significant commitments but chose instead to try to execute the agreement with the city rather than a coalition of community groups, arguing that the signatories needed to be entities sure to be around for decades into the future. The community groups put up a fuss, claiming they had been excluded from the process, and the mayor's office dragged its feet on approving the agreement. Meanwhile, Rice went ahead and built The Ion on schedule.

This, then, is the conundrum of economic development today. Places are improved by prosperity—indeed, places cannot thrive without prosperity because the two are deeply interconnected. But in a society with deepening inequality, places can also be overrun by prosperity. So how do you restore the balance between place and prosperity in a way that's equitable? This question goes to the most fundamental question about cities today: Can they truly be a vehicle for upward mobility? Or will they simply be a space shared by the rich and poor while middle-class folks— to the extent that they still exist—flee to the suburbs or even the exurbs?

The whole process of urbanization has always left some people behind. From time immemorial, people who lived in cities and towns, where high-value goods were made and traded, were more prosperous than those who lived in the countryside, where low-value agricultural products were grown. That's why urbanization is such a strong trend all over the world: Traditionally, there is more economic opportunity in cities than in the countryside.

The gentrification problem as we see it today is a little different. Except that today, those left behind are not in the countryside but in the city itself, adjacent to but not sharing in the prosperity the city is creating. And, understandably, it makes longtime residents mad.

The anti-gentrification approaches taken in recent years are important steps. But sometimes they seem like mere Band-Aids, simply mitigating the problem but not solving it. It is important, for example, to provide affordable housing that is not affected by changing market conditions that could make that housing unaffordable. But most people don't live in such subsidized housing, however; rather, they live in private housing built by the private market. For cities to work, their markets have to work, and in a world where some people have a lot of money and most people don't, it is very hard for markets to work properly.

All of which may suggest that, at least in the case of gentrification, a city—however marvelously complex and adaptable it is—is no match for broad-based social and economic inequality. Yes, cities are traditionally places of opportunity, and that opportunity must be shared as broadly as possible.

Efforts to ensure affordable housing and job opportunities for residents in long-neglected neighborhoods are vital to ensuring those neighborhoods remain vital and diverse in the future. But sometimes cities simply reveal social and economic trends by distributing those trends across the landscape. Income inequality is an endemic problem, deeply rooted in the US tax structure, the expectations of those who control capital, and the concentration of political and legal power among the traditionally places of opportunity, and that opportunity must be shared as broadly as possible. When inequality is an endemic problem, a city and its economic development efforts may be able to offer only Band-Aids—big Band-Aids that help, but Band-Aids nevertheless.

PART 3

THE PROMISED LAND

Because I have lived in Texas since moving there from California in 2014—and because there's such a fierce and not always good-hearted rivalry between the two states—I was at first reluctant to call out my experiences with and writing about California urbanism as a separate section in this book. But the more I thought about it, the more necessary it became to me.

I lived in California for more than thirty years—from my midtwenties to my late fifties—and more than anywhere else except Auburn, California has shaped my thinking about cities and urbanism. It was where I most comprehensively investigated the roots of how cities grow (with *The Reluctant Metropolis*), and it was where I tried to put my ideas about urbanism to work (during my time on the Ventura City Council).

It often seems these days that California is going through one of its periodic apocalyptic periods—political turmoil, a population decline, endless wildfires, stratospheric home prices. But as I point out in "The California Attitude," the state is nothing if not resilient. Perhaps most remarkable is the way it has been transformed from a suburban to an urban state during my adult life. California is by no means perfect—congested, expensive, unequal—but at its best, the Golden State still points the way to a better future for cities and the people who live in them.

CHAPTER 15

The Long Drive

If you define the Los Angeles megalopolis broadly enough, which most people are unwilling to do, I lived at one end of it. I lived in Ventura, shorthand for San Buenaventura. It's a working-class oil town turned typical Southern California suburb, located where Highway 101 hits the ocean after a sixty-five-mile trip north and west from downtown Los Angeles. LA's sprawl has crept toward Ventura along the 101 Corridor across the fertile, flat soil of the Oxnard Plain. It's blocked from moving farther by the Pacific and an imposing set of rugged hills up toward Santa Barbara known as the Rincon. In a very real sense, this is where Los Angeles ends.

Most of my neighbors didn't want to believe that we in Ventura were part of Los Angeles. A lot of them moved to Ventura or thereabouts to register a vote with their feet on how they feel about Los Angeles. The irony of this attitude is rich indeed. Geographically, Ventura is close. We watch LA's television shows and listened to its radio stations. Economically, Ventura and LA are linked, much more than they were in the oil boom days, when Ventura's strongest economic ties were to Bakersfield and Houston. And when something bad happened in LA—a fire, an earthquake, a riot—our friends and relatives called to make sure we were okay. Our response was usually that everything is fine because we don't really live there. We had decided that we live somewhere else. It should have come as no surprise to me, then, to learn that the people at the other end felt pretty much the same way.

I remember the day I found the other end. It was a moody, rainy morning in the spring of 1990, and I braved the freeways for three-plus hours in my 1977 Honda Civic to go to Moreno Valley in Riverside County. Skidding across wet lanes of the freeway—Southern Californians are terrible wet-weather drivers, treating every rainstorm as if it were a blizzard—I traveled through suburb after suburb, past shopping center after shopping center and tract after tract. Camarillo. Calabasas. Woodland Hills. Sherman Oaks. Studio City. Glendale. Pasadena. Duarte. San Dimas. Pomona. Corona. The suburban monotony was so continuous that it was numbing.

Then, after a hundred and thirty miles, I stopped and saw a meadow. Rich and green from the spring rains, hard up against the San Jacinto Mountains, this was obviously the edge of town. Roads trailed off into ruts. Houses had a ramshackle look, with old tools and cars in the yard. Retail establishments were made of cinder blocks. There are more towns past the mountains—Banning, Beaumont, Palm Springs—but nothing else I had seen that day conveyed quite the same sense of termination.

It had taken almost half a day, and I had covered a distance that would have taken me through three or four Northeastern states, but I had finally found the other end of Los Angeles. As I traveled around Moreno Valley that day, I found that the people I talked to felt as much alienation from Los Angeles as my neighbors did in Ventura.

Moreno Valley had grown in size from ten thousand people to more than one hundred thousand in less than a decade, and it was almost a parody of the typical 1980s suburb: subdivision after subdivision along the freeway, punctuated only by shopping centers and franchise

Moreno Valley in Riverside County, California
(Credit: Riverside Press Enterprise/Southern California New Group via Getty Images)

restaurants, all linked together by overgrown arterials that the traffic engineers had demanded up front. Mini-malls were so ubiquitous that they even housed churches, which had nowhere else to go. And even more than Ventura, Moreno Valley was dependent on the Los Angeles megalopolis. It was largely vacant during working hours, with a third of the breadwinners off in Los Angeles or Orange County or Riverside making the money they would import back to their Moreno Valley tracts. The trick for making the seventy-mile trip bearable, the long-distance commuters said, was to hit the critical interchange of Highway 60 and Highway 91—the main road to Orange County—before five in the morning, when it began to jam up. The interchange of Highway 60 and Highway 91 is fifty-six miles east of downtown Los Angeles.

And yet it was here, in this unlikely place on the desert's edge, that people said they found a semblance of community no longer available to them in Los Angeles or Lakewood or Fullerton or El Monte. Some combination of "low" prices for housing ($130,000 for a starter home at the time, in 1990), an illusion of spaciousness, and the old suburban ideal that everybody here was starting fresh had so much appeal that it seemed worth the hassle.

One local resident, who endured the two-hour commute to Orange County for several years, told me he could have found a house closer to his work, "but I wouldn't have been able to have a pool." A former flight instructor employed by a local developer who wanted to build more than three thousand houses and a business park (on that meadow I found) said he didn't really mind living in a half-built, auto-bound community in the middle of nowhere. In fact, he said, it made him nostalgic. It reminded him of his boyhood in Orange County thirty years earlier.

Given these attitudes, it should have been equally unsurprising that when a large portion of urban Los Angeles erupted in flames and riots almost exactly two years later, people in places like Ventura and Moreno Valley didn't think it had much to do with their lives or their communities.

Triggered by the acquittal of four White Los Angeles police officers accused of beating Black motorist Rodney King, the 1992 LA riots raged over an enormous area—a hundred square miles or more, an area bigger than most large US cities. The riot zone encompassed LA's historically Black neighborhoods, as well as dozens of other crowded districts that were entry points for recent immigrants from Asia, Mexico, and Central America. Many of the names were familiar enough to people anywhere in Southern California: Watts. Central Avenue. West Adams. USC and the Coliseum. Koreatown. MacArthur Park. Even Hollywood. But to the suburbanites watching the tragedy on television, most of these places were nothing more than names—poor, neglected places that had been thrown away, decades earlier, by their parents or grandparents. In the mental map of Southern California that most people carry around in their heads, the riot zone was a hole in the metropolitan doughnut.

The riots touched people in the outer suburbs. Most had a friend or relative in danger who had never escaped the urban detritus; many opened their homes to others during the riots. Older suburbanites remembered living and working in neighborhoods that were going up in flames. One friend, a woman in her fifties, said that watching the riots brought back vivid memories of crouching in her Wilshire District home during the Watts riots of 1965 while chaos reigned on the street outside. For her, the whole experience simply confirmed the wisdom of her decision to flee many years before to Camarillo, fifty miles away.

In the months and years that followed, there was considerable evidence that the riots had profoundly affected all of Southern California's suburbs and all of its suburbanites. In Ventura County, where I lived, Korean merchants arrived en masse from Los Angeles, looking for retail stores to operate without having to fear for their lives. They quickly learned that they needed a gun in a poor neighborhood in Oxnard just as much as in South Central LA. In Moreno Valley, where working-class Black neighborhoods had grown up around a local air force base, South Central kids arrived regularly, sent to live with aunts and uncles located far from the turmoil of urban life. The result, as Moreno Valley quickly discovered, was not a reduction of gang activity but a geographical expansion of it. (The gang member "Monster" Kody Scott, who wrote a well-publicized autobiography, divided his time between South Central and Moreno Valley and was arrested in Moreno Valley for beating up a man who allegedly derided his gang.) And all over Southern California—as the region reeled from a devastating recession and a series of natural disasters—businesses, workers, and families suffered from bad publicity worldwide.

Yet none of these events drew people together. If anything, they pushed them further apart. Nothing has changed in my neighborhood, people said; I have nothing to worry about. Maybe the people in South Central burned down each other's mini-malls, but in our town the chaos seemed about as real as the Gulf War. (The riots didn't come within thirty miles of Simi Valley, the conservative suburban enclave in Ventura County where the Rodney King trial was held.) Those who feared their neighborhoods were changing moved farther away, and those who were still afraid moved behind walls and gates where, they hoped, the rest of society couldn't follow. Even people who really did live in Los Angeles continued to atomize, bombarding the US Postal Service with requests to list their residences as being located in North Hills, West Hills, Sherman Valley, or anything but Los Angeles. (In 1996 and again in 2002, the San Fernando Valley even sought to secede from the City of Los Angeles.) Instead of trying to fix Los Angeles, we all simply decided that we live somewhere else.

That lush meadow I saw in Moreno Valley doesn't have three thousand houses and a business park on it today, as the developer of the property anticipated. In part that's because real estate and capital markets collapsed shortly after my visit. But it's also because, predictably, there was no consensus in Moreno Valley about what should be done. Many of the town's political leaders supported the project because the developer promised that businesses locating there would provide local jobs. But a lot of local homeowners, who thought that jobs would never materialize, did not want to chew up a beautiful meadow to build houses for a few more commuters competing for space on the freeway at 4:30 a.m.

I didn't stick around long enough to form a strong opinion one way or the other. By the end of the day it had stopped raining, so I got back into my Civic and headed west on the freeway. Moreno Valley was interesting, but it was just another suburb of Los Angeles. It wasn't really a part of where I live. It was too distant, too remote, too filled with cars and shopping centers and commuting suburbanites who didn't fit the ambiguously anti-urban image I had of the town where I live. Like everybody else in metropolitan Los Angeles, I just wanted to get home to my tract.

CHAPTER 16
The California Attitude

In the mid-1800s, the Golden Gate was a spectacular natural land formation—visible to passing sailors, unconnected by any handsome bridges of human creation, and serving as the entrance to one of the greatest natural estuaries in the world. At the start of 1849, San Francisco was a town of two thousand people, typically rowdy but barely intruding on the pristine and treeless peninsula on which it was located. California's vast Central Valley produced no food—at least not the kind of cultivated food that people all over the world put on their table every day—yet its multitude of rivers and wetlands supported a diversity of fish and wildlife unmatched anywhere else. The forests of the North Coast were almost untouched, producing, as they had for hundreds of years, some of the largest and most magnificent trees in creation. Southern California was a dusty, semi-arid land dotted with a few Roman Catholic missions that grew irrigated crops with the help of what remained of once-thriving tribes of Native Americans. Almost seven decades after its 1781 founding, Los Angeles remained quite literally a "cow town," deriving most of its wealth from cowhides and candle tallow made from cow fat. And underneath the flowing rivers and plentiful oak woodlands of the Sierra Nevada lay an unknown, untapped lode of the world's most precious metal.

Then the sluice gates opened, and down out of the Sierra Foothills poured gold. And not just a little gold, but such vast amounts of gold that it transformed California almost instantaneously into a modern society. Two years after gold was first discovered near a sawmill on the South Fork of the American River in 1848, California was delivering $10 million a year of the precious metal to the rest of the world. Two years after that, the figure had risen to $80 million, and California was producing most of the world's gold. As news of the gold strike spread, a staggering number of people arrived in search of their fortune. From a non-Native American population of about eight thousand at the time of the discovery, California grew to twenty thousand people the first year, one hundred thousand the second, and two hundred thousand by 1852, just four years after gold was first discovered. This great influx of humanity came from all over the world—from the East Coast, Hawaii, China, Ireland, and Germany—enhancing California's well-established status as a multicultural society.

But as the great California writer Carey McWilliams observed a half-century ago, however, the least important aspect of the entire story was probably the actual discovery and production of gold. Far more important was that gold gave California an immediate base of wealth unmatched in American history, and the Gold Rush quickly created a vast and affluent market for practically everything. More than one historian has pointed out that California benefited far more from the merchants and capitalists who fleeced the miners of their gold than from actually mining the golden fleece.

Within two years of the discovery at Sutter's Mill, gold gave California such political power that it leapfrogged over half the country to become a state. Within five years, it had generated such wealth that capitalists set up large-scale mining operations and began to squeeze out the little guys with their sluice boxes. And within a decade, gold had made San Francisco into one of the nation's leading cities, jump-starting its transformation into the only city west of St. Louis capable of financing the growth and development of the American frontier.

In other words, gold allowed California to simply bypass the long, slow process of agrarian development that other states had taken many decades to pass through. It generated the vast wealth required to unlock the massive potential of a rough but fragile region. Gold formed the basis for virtually every other aspect of California's early development. It hastened the exploration of the redwood forests and created a huge market for lumber products, thus stimulating the state's massive timber industry. It laid the foundation for California's vast agricultural industry by populating the Central Valley with thousands of would-be miners who saw farming as a more attractive long-term career. It even set the stage for the large-scale urban development of the twentieth century by forcing the creation of a sophisticated system for settling competing claims to large tracts of land.

More important, gold gave California a worldwide cache as a glamorous and exciting place where anything was possible. Little wonder that while other states adopted mottos like "Live Free or Die" and "Ever Upward," California's motto has always been "I Have Found It" ("Eureka")—the "it" meaning not only gold, but just about any limitless goal of human activity that seemed impossible to achieve anywhere else. "In California," McWilliams wrote at the time of the state's centennial in 1950, "the lights went on all at once, in a blaze, and they have never dimmed."

California has aptly been described as an island, sealed off from the rest of the world by deserts, mountains, and the Pacific Ocean. So complete is California's physical separation that—like Australia—it is a kind of self-contained biological experiment, full of plant and animal species found nowhere else in the world. California, according to Elna Bakker, a leading chronicler of California's natural communities, "has developed in its own way and at its own pace; evolutionary history here has woven numerous distinctive patterns of interaction between life form and the land." As a result, Bakker added, "Lichen-shrouded sea-mist forest is but an hour's drive from a mineral-encrusted dry lake. Prairie and the world's tallest forest are only a few feet apart." California's patterns "have similarities, but no exact duplicates elsewhere in the world." They are "incredibly intricate, multiple, and unfortunately irreplaceable."

After the Gold Rush, however, the explosive nature of the state's development quickly turned the island into a hothouse. Modern California was such a magnetic locale, formed so quickly and with such blistering intensity, that it fired the creation of a wholly different way of looking at the world—a viewpoint that can only be called the "California attitude."

Maybe the most basic component of the California attitude is the comfortable, almost casual manner in which Californians take the relentless velocity of their society in stride. Given the state's history, this nonchalance shouldn't be surprising. From the Gold Rush onward, the state's wealth and growth have occurred at warp speed. And so Californians are accustomed to operating in a fast-moving environment in which change itself is the only constant.

But the underlying terrain across which Californians move so quickly is a vast and magnificent canvas. Like most of the US West, California is at once dramatic and fragile. It is awe-inspiring in its scale and potential, and the variety of its natural resources is breathtaking—ranging from stark, rugged mountains to fertile valleys to unparalleled coastline. Yet California's resources are hard to crack open and easily damaged once the tampering begins. California's natural wonders have often left even its most ruthless developers speechless. "Almost the first thought passing in one's mind, as he enters a virgin forest of redwoods," wrote journalist and businessman Charles Goodwin Noyes in 1884, "is one of pity that such a wonderful creation of nature should be subject to the greed of man for gold." So rapt was Noyes by nature that he included these words in a book prepared especially to interest Eastern capitalists in investing in the California redwood industry.

This rare combination of velocity and scale means that Californians have always had an intense relationship with the landscape. By skipping over the agrarian phase of development, California also skipped the slow and agonizing process of taming the landscape—farm by farm, tree by tree, stump by stump—that characterized the rest of the United States. Thus, many parts of the state remain raw and wild. Even today, a new subdivision almost anywhere in the state is likely to intrude on an untamed landscape never before disturbed by humans.

We see this attitude play out every day on the waves and in the mountains through such distinctively California pastimes as surfing and mountain biking. These pastimes seek out an "in-your-face" encounter with nature, but they also try to soften and manage the experience with such modern inventions as wet suits and shock absorbers. A century before the invention of the wet suit, however, this jarring collision with nature—the manipulation of a resource with unprecedented speed and force—was already present in the California attitude.

When panning for gold no longer yielded results and digging for gold proved too difficult, enterprising Californians in the 1850s came up with a better idea. They discovered that they could save days of effort simply by hosing down the gravel hillsides of Nevada County with vast quantities of water—washing the mountains away and leaving the gold behind. Before long, "hydraulic mining" had become a capital-intensive business, producing large quantities of wealth with great efficiency by creating a jarring collision between Californians and nature.

It was the first of many capital-intensive, large-scale methods that Californians used to unlock the great potential that nature held for them. Though the process was extractive, the effect was almost miraculously transformative. Everywhere else in the West, the mining of precious metals created a boom-and-bust economy controlled by absentee owners. In California, it created indigenous wealth that stimulated cycle after cycle of transformation.

These transformations have taken many forms. Sometimes, they have been transformations of nature that helped build modern California—aqueducts, vast farms, railroads, and highways. Other times, the result has been a chain reaction of events unprecedented in human history. The Gold Rush, for example, helped create a powerful railroad, which in turn generated the wealth that allowed Leland Stanford to endow a great university, which in turn spawned the growth of Silicon Valley, which changed the world in a thousand different ways and brought more wealth back to California, to be recycled yet again—a millennium of change in only 150 years.

The message contained in such examples is clear: Over and over again, that jarring collision between California and nature has transformed California from a myth into a reality far beyond anything the myth could have promised. And in the process, it has reaffirmed the belief of most Californians in transformation as the foundation of their identity. After all this time in the hothouse, Californians believe they do not extract, they do not alter; they *transform*. They take what they have been given, manipulate it on a grand scale, and create something entirely new in the process.

California has paid a big price for this transformation, however. Jarring collisions with nature may be exhilarating—and profitable—but they are not always good for nature. And ironically, they often turn out to be bad for people too, at least in the long run. California's history—and its present-day landscape—are quite literally littered with testaments to this relentless equation.

Hydraulic mining, for example, turned out to be a threat to the very people who profited from it. The Sacramento Valley town of Marysville grew prosperous manufacturing the arterial-style "monitors" that were used to hammer the hillsides with water. It wasn't long, however, before the debris shaken loose by this artillery came barreling back down the Feather River, threatening the existence of the town where the equipment that dislodged the debris was made.

Nor is that the end of the story. More than a century after hydraulic mining was halted in California, the debris is still flowing down the Feather and Sacramento Rivers, raising the water level significantly. Marysville must still protect itself with levees that wall the town off from the outside world. Sacramento, now a metropolis of a million people, is the most flood-prone large city in the United States. And landowners up and down the Sacramento Valley are still suing one another over who should be responsible.

When hydraulic mining finally was halted, it wasn't because of the environmental devastation the process wreaked. It was because the rising waters of the Feather and Sacramento Rivers threatened another great transforming manipulation of nature: the cultivation of the Central Valley. The agriculture industry had its own sweeping effect on California's growth, and it has created its own environmental backlash by depriving the Sacramento–San Joaquin Delta of the flushes of freshwater needed for wildlife to survive there. Just as an explosive chain of events has led from the Gold Rush to modern-day Silicon Valley, so too have chain reactions of environmental side effects built upon one another in California until they have reached monumental proportions.

Thus the raw and intense relationship between Californians and their landscapes cuts both ways. Only in California would somebody dream up the transforming idea of simply hosing a mountain out of existence in order to gather the gold left behind. Only in California, with its fragile ecology, would it have been possible to find mountains that would evaporate under the pressure of a strong stream of water. Only in California would the result have been such an environmental disaster, leaving behind remnants that still cause problems today. And only in California would the whole mess be shut down simply because it interfered with another jarring collision of nature.

Given all that, it is perhaps not surprising that California's environmentalists also have an intense relationship with nature. These environmentalists have always been created in the same hothouse-type environment as the capitalists who developed the state's natural resources, and the result is equally unalloyed. To a California environmentalist, it is not enough to manage nature responsibly and harvest a sustainable bounty, Gifford Pinchot–style. To combat the jarring and exploitative collision with a fragile environment like California's, you must defend nature with your very life—lay down in front of a bulldozer, tie yourself to a rock, or at least seek a stay of execution in court with the fervor of a public defender desperately trying to save the life of a death-row murderer.

This brand of environmentalism has been exported worldwide since the 1970s. California is widely credited with creating and shaping the modern environmental movement, especially after the Santa Barbara oil spill of 1969, which focused the nation's attention on environmental problems. Like the debris flowing down the Feather River toward Marysville, the oil flowing toward the California coastline served as a testament to the notion that colliding with nature cuts both ways and that the very resources that have allowed California to prosper can swallow it as well.

The resulting approach to environmental protection, with its focus on heavy regulations, bears the unmistakable imprint of the California attitude. If the jarring collision with nature can create legacies like hydraulic mining and offshore drilling, the reasoning went, then only an equally uncompromising response can prevent further damage.

Oddly, for a society that has always prided itself on moving so rapidly across open ground, California also has a national reputation for sheer density. The hothouse environment that enabled the state to grow so fast has also incubated laws, regulations, and vested interests more quickly than anywhere else in the West and possibly in the nation. It is hard to move, at least in the political or economic arena, without tripping over something or somebody that can hold you back.

In part, this conflict stems from California's peculiar history as a self-reliant region that has faced the bureaucratic attempts of three different nations to lasso it. Even before the Gold Rush, California was a welter of conflicting claims on land and natural wealth. Then, gold's quick riches instantly created a plethora of vested economic interests, all noisily jostling with one another for advantage. Throughout the twentieth century, California saw the construction of large-scale public works projects—waterworks, freeways, and so on—that have altered the natural environment for the benefit of these economic interests. And, at the same time, the state saw wave after wave of populist regulation—environmental regulation included—designed to rein in the economic interests.

This historical sequence has quite literally shaped the modern California landscape: the raw exploitation, the massive alteration, and finally the desperate counterreaction to save what is left. The result is a society that has gotten better at making sure that bad things don't happen to the natural environment as easily as they used to.

Yet merely preventing the further destruction of California's natural bounty is not enough anymore. After decades of colliding with nature, California is paying a heavy price that is likely to get more burdensome before it gets lighter. All that debris rolling down the Feather and Sacramento Rivers serves as an apt metaphor for the lasting, and still harmful, imprint that California's prosperous society has left on the state's legendary landscapes. Even if we do nothing more to our environment—level no more mountains, divert no more water, extract nothing more from the earth—we will still be left with the fallout of the golden legacy for decades, if not centuries, to come.

CHAPTER 17

The Not-So-Reluctant Metropolis

Shortly after *The Reluctant Metropolis* was released in 1997, I was giving a lecture to a small group of people in a private home on the Westside of Los Angeles—this is the sort of thing authors do in hopes of selling books—when a skeptical listener disarmed me with a question I hadn't considered.

I had just concluded my standard litany about L.A. The entire metropolis, I argued, had hunkered down into a destructive cycle of "cocoon citizenship." People were divided, not united, by the metropolis; they had no sense of regional identity and no sense of common destiny. The 1992 riots and the natural disasters that followed had made this situation worse, not better, and Angelenos needed to find common ground in order to restore a healthy balance of both citizenship and community. But this listener was not persuaded.

"So," she asked, in a somewhat sardonic tone, "are you saying that L.A. is somehow fundamentally *different* from any other city?"

She clearly expected me to say yes. But much to her surprise—and, indeed, my own—I found myself saying no. My point about Los Angeles was right, I insisted. Its citizens *were* wrapping themselves up inside cocoons. But this was most assuredly not unique. And that was the most important point I was trying to make in *The Reluctant Metropolis*: It may, on the surface, tell stories from Los Angeles, but it is really about the conundrum of current metropolitan life in the United States.

When I first arrived in Los Angeles in 1981, I approached it as an alien object, much as an astronaut, encased in a spacesuit, might cautiously poke at moonrocks on the barren lunar landscape. Over time, however, I came to realize that, far from being alien, Los Angeles is in fact the most American of cities. It is, in a phrase, just like any other American city only more so—more sprawling, more vibrant, more xenophobic, more rich, more poor, more selfish, more caring. From Bell Gardens to Bellflower to Bel-Air, it encompasses everything, good and bad, about people trying to make the American Dream work for them in the modern, oversized metropolis.

At the same time, however, there is no denying that L.A. is different in degree if not in kind. The problems of regional identity that afflict every American metropolis—the problems that separate cities from suburbs, rich from poor—are accentuated by L.A.'s geography and by the way that city has developed in response to that geography. It is divided by mountains rather than connected by water or some other natural feature. The test of Los Angeles is whether it can build and sustain a common sense of identity as it matures and diversifies.

Since *The Reluctant Metropolis* was first published, I have also realized that the situation I described is not static but, rather, dynamic. For example, immigration to Los Angeles and suburban flight from it are both important themes in the book. Yet during the recession that wracked L.A. in the mid-1990s and during the subsequent economic boom, I was surprised to discover that both these phenomena have ebb and flow and even evolve in ways we wouldn't expect. During the recession, Mexicans went back to Mexico because the jobs dried up, and Moreno Valleyites went back to Orange County because home prices went down. (Later, of course, the patterns ebbed and flowed again as prices rose.) People may make arduous and seemingly illogical life choices at a given moment in time, but they don't do so with the intention of retaining those lifestyles forever. They keep expecting things to get better—at least for themselves, if not for the metropolis as a whole.

As the recession gave way to the new economic boom in the late 1990s, the mood around the region changed dramatically. The gloomy pall that pervaded the place after the riots, fires, and earthquakes lifted, and people began to feel good again. Understandable though this may be, I fear that it might be only temporary. Many of the problems I described in *The Reluctant Metropolis*—greed, narrow-mindedness, an unwillingness to sacrifice for the common good, a reluctance to see the destiny of the region as a common one—are characteristic of a place that has passed through a pimply adolescence and is now settling into complacent middle age.

In 1980, approximately the point at which *The Reluctant Metropolis* begins to tell its story of metropolitan Los Angeles, the five-county L.A. region was home to 7 million Anglos and 4 million people of other races. Twenty years later, metro L.A. still had 7 million Anglo residents. But it was also home to 9 million people of other races—mostly Latino and Asian groups, whose numbers have doubled and tripled, respectively, in the intervening years. In other words, during the period that *The Reluctant Metropolis* covers, Los Angeles became a dramatically different place—one far more multiethnic and multicultural than it was before. *The Reluctant Metropolis* is not really the story of how this new metropolis emerged, so much as it is the story of the last wretched gasps of the Anglo suburban one that preceded it.

Perhaps the most striking change since this book was first published is the way in which this change in demographics has finally stimulated a remarkable rise in grassroots Latino political power. By the late 1990s, Latinos began turning out in large numbers for bigger elections and quickly established themselves as a major force for social conservativism, law-and-order, good schools, and other staples of working-class upward mobility. Mayor Richard Riordan owed a good portion of his easy victory over Tom Hayden in 1997 to the fact that he got seventy percent of the Latino vote. The Los Angeles Unified School District obtained the required two-thirds vote to pass a $2.4 billion bond issue mostly because Latinos turned out in force and favored the bond measure by 80-20. Antonio Villaraigosa, a former "street kid" from East Los Angeles, emerged as the speaker of the California Assembly and mayor of L.A. Latinos now dominate Los Angeles politics.

The sudden appearance of Latino voters led to a battle over their hearts and souls in Los Angeles. Despite their social conservatism, most Latino voters emerged as Democrats—in large part because Governor Pete Wilson so deeply alienated them with his support of Proposition 187, which denied public education to children living illegally in the state.

Riordan was a Republican, and he had been elected in 1993 on the strength of post-riot Anglo voters from the San Fernando Valley. However, like many other big-city mayors, he was a moderate Republican with strong ties to many Democrats. He had, after all, first risen to prominence as a confidant of Tom Bradley, the city's longtime African American mayor. But by late in his second term, as Latino politicians of all ideological stripes battled for power all around him, Riordan began to seem like an anachronism. It was clear that the future of L.A. politics—not just the city's, but maybe the region's as well—belonged to the Latinos.

Yet this very rise in Latino political influence seemed to increase the desire of the old Anglo metropolis to wall itself off from the emerging reality. Even more than most American metro areas, the gap between the haves and have-nots had grown dramatically in Los Angeles, due in large part to the vaunted class in L.A. of the First World and Third World economies. The recession of the early 1990s finished off the middle-class economy, which was based on the aerospace industry and traditional unionized factory jobs. In its place rose a two-tiered recovery, one tier based on high-end, high-tech jobs being created in high-amenity suburbs like Thousand Oaks and Irvine, and the other based on low-end apparel and manufacturing in the old Rust Belt of Southeast Los Angeles.

Research showed that immigrants were still able to climb the ladder of mobility once they were here. But the continued immigration from Asia and Latin America—and, more important, the growing families in these immigrant communities, which now made up most of Southern California's population growth—made it *seem* to both liberals and conservatives that the have-nots were now dominating a once-suburban region. Anglos left north Orange County—to which they had fled from the Watts riots of 1965—and thriving Latino, Vietnamese, and other ethnic enclaves grew up in their place. The same was true in the San Gabriel Valley, in Burbank and Glendale, and even in distant neighborhoods in Riverside and Ventura counties.

The walling-off impulse, mostly on the part of affluent Anglos, did not decelerate. If anything, it grew. Several new municipalities were created, especially in southern Orange County, and virtually all of them were high-end white suburbs. In 1998, voters in Ventura County approved a series of ballot initiatives designed to prevent sprawling urban growth; though their proponents called it a farmland protection initiative, there was little doubt, as one letter to the editor put it, that part of the motivation was to "rid the county of excess people."

If the experience of other cities is any guide, it would seem that Angelenos will have to wait until they feel the slow and agonizing slide before they snap out of their delirium. This has certainly been the case in New York, Cleveland, and any number of other cities that spent decades denying their urban problems before they began to address them. Matched as a place to escape urban problems, L.A. may have a tougher time than most in shedding its cocoon-citizenship tendencies. Yet maybe Los Angeles will surprise us.

The most amazing thing about L.A. is the way it retains its youthful vibrancy. After a century of striving, Los Angeles is a rich, powerful, and mature place that can make a legitimate claim to being the most important metropolis on earth. It's even beginning to have old money. Paradoxically, however, L.A retains a raw energy so palpable that you can feel it just by walking—or, more accurately, driving—down the street. It's an energy that sizzles equally in the crowded immigrant districts and the tony neighborhoods. It's the most endearing and exciting quality this sprawling metropolis has, and to be perfectly honest I can't quite figure out why it persists. But thank goodness it's there.

So maybe Los Angeles will succeed in producing, at least, a civic culture that is both enervating and enduring—one that can serve as the foundation for the very kind of regional citizenship and sense of common destiny so obviously lacking in *The Reluctant Metropolis*. This would be an unexpected development, of course. But even today, anything is possible in L.A. Which is not something you can say about every reluctant metropolis you ran across.

CHAPTER 18

Living the 2 Percent Life

A region as large and complicated as Southern California—nineteen million people spread across 191 jurisdictions covering thousands of square miles—is not powered by any one single force. What happens there is the result of a combination of economic, cultural, and political forces all across the globe and how those forces manifest themselves at home. When you think about the way in which Southern California has been affected since the 1970s by war throughout the world, the economic rise of East Asia, the end of the Cold War, the decline of the aerospace industry, and economic and political strife in Latin America—well, it's hard to imagine that regional efforts to manage growth are worth thinking about at all.

But regions do rise and fall in large part based on the policy decisions by their civic and political leaders. The original rise of Southern California as an urban power in the early part of the twentieth century was due in large part to such decisions—decisions to import water to the region and to build a vast regionwide transportation system capable of accommodating lots of additional growth.

Southern California is trying to envision anew what the region's future might look like and struggling to find ways to make that new vision become a reality. As is typical of the region, this new "visioning" effort is taking place in many different locations and venues around the region.

Such efforts originally took place through the Compass project, a regional growth visioning exercise undertaken by the Southern California Association of Governments (SCAG) that has used a variety of outreach methods, including public opinion surveys, workshops, and media articles. But it also takes place at the subregional level and in many city halls and county halls of administration throughout the region, to say nothing of civic and nonprofit organizations' visioning efforts and attempts by chambers of commerce and other business groups to get a hold on the region's future.

Southern California's need to rethink its future has emerged clearly from its demographic and economic changes—the decline of the postwar middle-class suburban dream and the rise of a more multiethnic, postindustrial society. Curiously, though, the regional planning visioning effort didn't come from Southern California at all. Rather, it came from a more classically suburban and homogeneous area—Salt Lake City—where a civic group formed by Utah's Governor Michael Leavitt and business leaders known as "Envision Utah" engineered a regional planning exercise in the late 1990s.

The biggest breakthrough to emerge from Envision Utah was what has come to be known as the "chip game." You get civic, political, and business leaders around a table with a map of the region, you give them "chips" that represent increments of future growth (in Salt Lake City, the "chips" were squares of paper), and you tell them to put the chips down where they think the growth should go.

In the introduction to our book *The Regional City*, Peter Calthorpe and I described how Leavitt (who later became administrator of the US

Environmental Protection Agency) and other leaders initially laid the chips down next to each other, consuming all agricultural land and scenic mountain plateaus. Then, realizing that this move will destroy open land they value, Leavitt and his colleagues began laying the chips on top of each other and on top of existing urban areas—in locations that were either underbuilt or in need of renewal.

The chip game was part of the foundation of SCAG's Compass project, which was designed to create a regional consensus about where future growth in Southern California might go and how it would be accommodated. But translating a technique developed in Salt Lake City to Southern California caused a few understandable bumps in the road. At 1.6 million people, metro Salt Lake was one-tenth the size of the SCAG region at the time—indeed, it's about the size of a SCAG subregion. And in such a big region with so many areas oriented toward a slow-growth approach, it's tempting just to put the chips in your pocket and pretend they don't exist—or else push them so far away from your neighborhood or town that your life will be unaffected, even though somebody's life might be seriously messed up as a result. That's the typical outcome of California's regional housing plan process, not just in Southern California but throughout the state, and it is exactly what happened in some of the Compass workshops.

But what also happened was an increased understanding that we're all in this together and future growth has to go somewhere. And although we might continue to fight about where growth will go—and how much of it will go here or there—most civic and political leaders in the region have now bought into SCAG's "2 percent strategy." This idea suggests that by focusing most growth on 2 percent of the land mass of the region—mostly in centers and corridors and near transit stops—we can accommodate most future growth in ways that strengthen and reinforce the region rather than make it more unmanageable.

The 2 percent strategy might seem pretty far-fetched at first, but it's really just an acknowledgment of the great urban design defect of Southern California, which is a lack of what might be called "centeredness."

In the early twentieth century, the Red Car system of interurban rails created a string of pearls from Santa Monica to San Bernardino—town centers that were compact, walkable, and diverse. Dozens of town centers were created, from Pasadena to Huntington Park to Laguna Beach to Ventura. Since the 1920s, however, most of Southern California's growth has focused on the automobile. For most of that time, the urban landscape of the region became more and more attenuated, and the compact centers, little by little, withered away.

By any measure, such sprawl is the biggest problem in the region. According to academics Reid Ewing and Rolf Pendall, along with smart growth advocate Don Chen, sprawl has four components: low population density, a lack of diversity at the neighborhood scale, a street system that is not connected, and a lack of strong downtowns and town centers.

Surprisingly, they found that most of Southern California—especially the coastal counties—scored very well on the first three components. Population density is high and getting higher—a function partly of household size but also because the region is not characterized by low-density subdivisions. (It's also partly because open-space efforts are creating a de facto urban growth boundary around the region, thus driving urban densities up.) The typical neighborhood contains a vast array of businesses and services—even if they are not always easily accessible on foot. And, thanks to superior planning in the suburban era, the idea of an interconnected street system is deeply embedded in most of the region.

Downtowns and town centers, on the other hand, are not nearly as strong here as they are elsewhere in the United States. The researchers found that Orange County, for example, ranked sixth out of eighty-three metropolitan areas in density, fifth in street connectivity, thirteenth in neighborhood mix—and seventy-third in centeredness. Results for Los Angeles and Ventura Counties were similar. Even Riverside/San Bernardino—the most sprawling area in the United States by far, according to the study—was in the middle of the pack on density but ranked eighty-first out of eighty-three areas in centeredness.

So how do we recapture our centeredness—how do we find and strengthen those city and town cores that serve as the focal point of the region's growth in the future? Conceptually, it isn't hard to do, though the practical politics can be tricky.

We know where these centers are. They include the unparalleled collection of old suburban downtowns with which Southern California, owing the Red Car days, has been endowed. They include suburban-era centers that are quickly morphing into something more than office districts or business parks—places like Valencia Town Center, Century City, and Irvine Spectrum. And they include the old commercial strips and dead malls—the vast expanse of obsolete retail land so vital in the 1950s or 1960s but unable to compete today with Nordstrom or Walmart.

The "how" is obvious as well. The problem of centeredness is not particularly a problem of office or retail space or even industrial land—at least not in Southern California, where most of these activities are already crammed together in close proximity. The problem of centeredness is, in a word, a problem of housing. Solving that problem requires nothing less than a revolution in the way we think about how our communities are constructed.

There's a general consensus in the United States that housing is the key to social stability, and—extremely important given the region's vast working class—it's one of the keys to upward mobility as well. In Southern California, though, it's also the key to centeredness.

The most important reason is that the vast majority of urban land—up to 70 percent in many cases—is used for housing. A region can be sprawling or not. It can be auto-oriented or focused, at least in some locations, on a transit system. It can have strong centers or not. But whatever this form is, it depends in large part on what type of housing is built and how it is distributed across the landscape.

Housing is important for another reason, too: It is the hottest sector in the real estate development market right now. Developers and urban landowners who were looking at office towers in the 1980s and entertainment retail in the 1990s are now looking at small-lot single-family subdivisions, townhomes, and condominiums.

More and more people are choosing to live in crowded and expensive urban areas—sometimes out of economic necessity, sometimes to avoid a wearying commute, and sometimes even as a lifestyle choice.

〰

One of these people was me. After sixteen years of living in a typical suburban 1960s tract house, I moved to historic downtown Ventura. It was quite a transition. One of the things I would often say when I gave speeches about how Southern California was changing is that, over time, people are going to have to acclimate themselves to a more urban lifestyle—something that many suburbanites can't even visualize.

I tried to do this in Ventura, but it was not all upside. I love easy access to transit, but I had a hard time sleeping when the buses started rumbling by about 5:30 a.m. every day. The police visited my block every once in a while, and homeless people wandered by on a regular basis. I lost a beloved dog to a traffic accident that probably wouldn't have occurred in a more quiet suburban setting. And it also took some getting used to the idea that my fourteen-year-old daughter could just yell, "See ya!" and be off to some store or shop on her own.

But I could walk to my local farmers' market, and the ten-screen movie theater was just past the library. Even my elected responsibilities were only four blocks away at the city hall. Sometimes a couple of days could pass without me getting in my car, and I didn't even notice it. And the skittishness in letting my daughter out into the world on her own was only part of the equation. I also had a sense of both relief and pride that she could gradually learn to navigate the world on her own, little by little – rather than all at once when I handed her the car keys.

These are the benefits a more urban lifestyle confers. They're not, from a suburban way of thinking, conventional benefits; in fact, many people would probably not consider them to be benefits at all. But they represent something different, and they are benefits not just to me, but to the community and even the entire region.

Simply building higher-density housing willy-nilly will not, in and of itself, provide these benefits. Part of the 2 percent strategy is not just confining new growth to 2 percent of the land, but knowing *which* 2 percent to focus on. And this is the revolutionary part, because traditional downtowns and town centers—even the beloved small suburban centers of Southern California—were not places where people traditionally lived.

As MIT professor Robert Fogelson pointed out in his excellent book *Downtown*, the emergence of the American downtown between 1880 and 1920 was based on the opposite premise: that a downtown was exclusively a business district where nobody lived. Businesses were centralized in downtown, while residents were dispersed in suburban districts. There may have been flophouses and declining working-class districts on the outskirts, but to gather the vast number of people required as workers and shoppers, downtowns depended not on local housing, but on modern transportation systems, especially trolleys.

So when we talk these days about creating vibrant town centers by building housing, we are not talking about the way things used to be. We are talking about a revolution: inserting housing into districts that, historically, were used exclusively for offices and stores.

Sometimes the process of revitalizing a retail downtown in a traditional way can morph, oddly, into the creation of a town center focused around housing. The revival of Old Town Pasadena began in the early 1990s as an effort to revive a deteriorated retail district by leveraging strategically positioned parking garages. Now Pasadena has evolved, improbably enough, into a second wave of urban renaissance that is focused on transit-oriented housing. Old Town became such a compelling destination that a housing market emerged, driven at least partly by the construction of the Gold Line light-rail system. Now the commercial buildings of the 1920s and the civic masterpieces of the City Beautiful era are punctuated by such twenty-first-century wonders as apartments built on top of a 1970s shopping mall and condominiums constructed, quite literally, over the tracks of a light-rail station.

If the 2 percent strategy is going to succeed, these are the kinds of places we have to focus on. Densifying 2 percent of the region won't do any good if it's just any 2 percent—that is, whatever 2 percent of the land that developers happen to gain control of and think they see a market for. Instead, we have to target the 2 percent of the land that includes places that can serve as true focal points—places that can accommodate more growth and can use that growth to shape a different and more urban kind of place.

If there is one other lesson from Envision Utah and other regional planning efforts, it is the challenge of implementation. For local elected officials, moving chips around on a big map of the region does not readily translate into downzoning someone's property on a Monday night to protect open space, or upzoning land in a promising center when you are confronted with a group of angry neighbors.

And herein lies a risk—a risk that Southern California's new more urban lifestyle, focused around new development in the region's vibrant centers, will somehow be maldistributed across the landscape. It seems likely, for example, that densification will occur mostly in two types of locations.

The first is the affluent area—already somewhat dense—where the economics of densification are so overpowering that developers will conclude that it is well worth fighting all the political fights to get a project through. This is the story of Pasadena, of the Westside of Los Angeles, of Santa Monica, the beach towns in Orange County.

The second is the working-class town that is already being overwhelmed by population growth—the older suburbs of southern Los Angeles and north Orange County and in the sliver of land in between the 10 and 60 Freeways in the San Gabriel Valley. In these towns, the usual political opposition to more housing dissipates somewhat, because local politicians can see they are getting the people whether the houses are built or not.

The hard part, as always, is the batch of small, affluent suburbs capable of putting both money and political power behind resisting growth. These towns are usually the flashpoints of regional growth debate—and, in particular, the pockets of resistance to the Regional Housing Needs Assessment process. The political reality is that growth will be distributed based on the mixture of political tolerance and economic pressure.

But the 2 percent strategy holds the potential to move beyond the stalemate, especially if it focuses on locations that have true potential to become transit-oriented centers. A few of the centers are located in the pockets of resistance, but not many. Most are located in exactly the places where growth is flowing anyway—the affluent areas where the political battle is worth it to the developers and the working-class locations where the population is growing. The 2 percent strategy will work if we let growth flow where political and economic forces are driving it anyway, but focus it tightly on centers that hold the potential for truly urban living. This has proven to be a huge struggle, especially in the affluent suburbs that resist more housing. But it's worth the fight.

CHAPTER 19

My Los Angeles

I arrived in Los Angeles for the first time in the early 1980s. Although I had traveled overland across most of the United States without a car on a typical peripatetic postcollegiate trip, a friend of mine in Phoenix talked me into flying the last leg west. I had never been to California before—indeed, I had only traveled west of the Mississippi once in my life, to attend my brother's college graduation in New Mexico when I was nine.

As the plane descended toward Los Angeles International Airport, I looked out the window northward and saw the familiar iconic images of the city: the Hollywood sign, downtown, the row of skyscrapers along Wilshire Boulevard. But that wasn't what mesmerized me. What really caught my attention were the miles and miles of wide arterials—Western, Normandie, Vermont—stretching southward from the Hollywood Hills to Long Beach, and the endless neighborhoods tucked between them: A seemingly endless flat plain filled with a seemingly endless grid and endless bungalows and small apartments.

This was the ordinary Los Angeles you saw, almost anonymously, in endless television shows and movies—the LA of *Dragnet* and *Adam-12*,

Aerial view of Los Angeles, California *(Credit: David Ramos/Creative Commons)*

where police cars roam endlessly through suburban-style neighborhoods dealing with urban-style crime. The great urbanist Reyner Banham called these neighborhoods the "Plains of Id," where ordinary people lived in ordinary neighborhoods and yet pursued self-fulfillment in a distinctly California way.

Today when I fly into LAX, the Plains of Id are still there, and with a more practiced eye I can pick out important punctuations on the landscape: Pacific Boulevard in Huntington Park; the White-turned-Latino downtown I wrote about in *The Reluctant Metropolis*; the Faith-Dome megachurch in South Central Los Angeles; the sad remnants of the once-fabulous Forum in Inglewood, where the Lakers played for decades. Yet, like the Forum, the city I came to know in the 1980s—my LA, if you will—sometimes seems to be just a distant memory.

Los Angeles was still largely White and middle class then, and neither

the politicians nor the policy wonks had quite caught on to the profound demographic change that was occurring at the time because of
what has come to be known as the Latino baby boom. There was no rail
transit—the transit chief spent most of his time inside the Beltway, lob-
bying for subway money—although the freeways and buses were both
very congested. The idea that Orange County was an urban center of its
own and not just a suburb was big news. The only funky older neighborhoods being gentrified were near the beach, not inland. The idea of
hipsters living downtown seemed like a cool idea, but one that would
never actually happen. Oh, yes, and the Dodgers—then still owned by
the O'Malley family—won the World Series twice.

Los Angeles has gotten both worse and better since then. It's much
more crowded—not just on the freeways, which are more congested
than ever, but also on surface streets and in many older neighborhoods
that serve as ports of entry for immigrant groups. Despite the success
of glitzy businesses like entertainment and high tech, Los Angeles has
struggled economically since the 1990s; it's a much more blue-collar
town than it used to be, with hundreds of thousands of people stuck in
low-paying, go-nowhere jobs.

Orange County has emerged as a powerful employment center that
rivals San Francisco in size. There's also much more sprawl, especially
out past Riverside and in the High Desert north of San Bernardino.
Mike Davis's dystopian vision in *City of Quartz*—that Southern California's sprawl has led to huge social dysfunction—is not entirely wrong.

Yet Los Angeles is a much better city as well, growing gradually and
comfortably into an urbanity worthy of its status as a world city. Sure,
it's still largely car-bound and horizontal, with employment centers
all over the place and dead-stop traffic jams in all directions. But for
the first time in many decades, it's a place where you can live without
a car and not feel like a second-class citizen. The great 1920s office
buildings downtown have been renovated as lofts. The hipsters live

not only downtown but in Koreatown. The largely Latino Eastside has been connected back to the rest of the city by the opening of the Gold Line Extension.

Today, LA is seeing high-end urban development at the rail transit stops—and more transit being built at a furious pace. Homeowner associations on the affluent Westside no longer fight to keep the subway out; now they fight to bring it in. Thanks to the pre-automobile structure created by the interurban rail system, no metropolis in the United States has such a large and wonderfully rich set of small downtowns, not just in Los Angeles, but in Orange County and the Inland Empire as well. And most of them are coming back as delightful places to live, work, and walk.

Around the time I arrived, the *Los Angeles Times* published a special magazine to commemorate Los Angeles's two hundredth anniversary (the city was founded in 1781). I still remember the featured essay by the legendary writer and activist Carey McWilliams. McWilliams, whose memory of Los Angeles stretched back to the 1920s, called it "a very special city in spite of itself"—meaning that it had emerged as an urban place despite its deeply engrained suburban mindset.

Today, we can celebrate the fact that we have moved beyond that place. Los Angeles is no longer an accidental city or a reluctant metropolis. Yes, it's got problems. It's never fully recovered its middle class, and like the rest of California, it is now burdened by astronomical home prices. But it has finally grown out of its pimply adolescence and matured into a world-class urban place.

CONCLUSION

On the Morning after the Pandemic

As I write this conclusion, I am sitting on the sofa in our home office in midtown Houston, locked down during the COVID-19 pandemic. I'm about as far away from Gary Kromer's Syracuse University dorm room, in geography and time and cultural orientation, as it's possible to imagine and still be in the contiguous United States. Houston's a place I never in a million years expected to live. It has a reputation as America's uncity—a mostly suburban, shapeless place, ironically similar to how we used to think of Los Angeles, which is another city where I never expected to live. Yet I am surrounded by most of the miracles of everyday city life.

Despite my fear of walking these days—partly because of my eyesight, partly because of the way Houstonians drive—for me it is a short and easy walk to most of the things I need on a daily basis, including restaurants, the drugstore, and even Houston's most prominent liquor store. We live one mile away from Minute Maid Park, where the Astros play, and Toyota Center, where the Rockets play and Beyoncé sings. It is three miles to work at Rice University.

Indeed, living without a car and the ability to drive, I often reflect on how I manage to get around. I use the light-rail train, which runs on six-minute headways, and the bus, which runs on fifteen-minute headways. I use Uber and Lyft on a regular basis. Before I stopped driving, I regularly traveled and shopped using Zipcar, a by-the-hour car rental service with many locations in my neighborhood. For my regular business trips to Austin, the state capital, I have my choice of several private intercity bus services, all of which begin their trip within walking distance of my house.

Quite literally, none of these options existed at the start of this century—not even the fifteen-minute headways for the bus. As a city-oriented person to begin with, and now one who cannot drive, I could not have lived the life I now have as recently as 2000. The miracle of cities—indeed, the miracle of *place*—works to my advantage even here in Houston, seemingly the most suburban of cities.

Nobody really knows how the coronavirus pandemic will affect cities—how they will affect places and their prosperity. At first, there was a lot of talk about how urban residents were fleeing to "Zoomburbs" and "Zoomtowns," suggesting that cities were "over." At the same time, for reasons nobody can quite explain, the real estate market went nuts, with home prices increasing by 25 percent and more during a year when nobody went anywhere and a lot of economy activity—especially retail and restaurant activity—dried up. You would think that prices would go down in San Francisco while going up in Walnut Creek, Lake Tahoe, and Boise. But the truth is that prices went up everywhere.

At the same time, retail businesses, restaurants, and bars—the business sectors that provide life and breath to busy city streets—were shut down for a long time, and many didn't make it to the end of the pandemic. Public transit systems, which provide a lifeline of mobility to people in cities, cut way back, and some were on the verge of going under.

There's no question that urban life throughout the United States will be permanently changed as a result of the pandemic. Major business districts that rely on office workers will shrink—or they may have to reinvent themselves, adding a more diverse set of activities to continue prospering. Old office buildings may flip to hotel or residential use. Suburban shopping centers will have big cavities where retail stores used to exist, and those vacancies will not be filled anytime soon. Maybe half as many people will ride public transit as before, which will put a strain on those who are transit-dependent while filling the streets with more Uber and Lyft vehicles patronized by more affluent urbanites.

Yet at the same time, as more and more people were vaccinated and ventured out in the world, however, it became clear that they missed cities and, in particular, places where they could gather and socialize. That's why outdoor dining in places like Main Street in Ventura, which I described earlier in this book, became so instantly popular. Yes, a lot of restaurants and bars have gone bankrupt. But the restaurant and bar scene—the lifeblood of a city's social life—will come roaring back.

But even as the affluent fled places like New York City and San Francisco, they didn't move just anywhere. They moved to specific locations—smaller cities, yes, but ones that provided the same kind of urban amenities they had left behind, such as restaurants, breweries, parks, hiking trails, and gathering places. Recently, my daughter and her family made this exact kind of move, leaving Berkeley for a new home in Bend, Oregon, which supposedly has more breweries per capita than any other city in the United States.

I recently flew on a Friday from San Francisco to the closest airport to Bend, in Redmond, Oregon, and everyone on the flight knew everyone else—they were all tech workers commuting to their home offices after a brief visit to headquarters in Silicon Valley. You don't have to be Enrico Moretti or Richard Florida to know what happens next: tech workers sitting in their spare bedrooms in Bend begin to start companies and raise venture capital out of Silicon Valley. The *locations* may change, but there's still a strong connection between high-amenity places and emerging prosperity.

So if you're lucky enough to be able to afford a high-amenity urban life—whether it's in midtown Houston, where I live, or Bend, where my daughter lives—cities still give you everything you need. But during the pandemic, I have come to realize how lucky I am to be able to live this life—and how, increasingly, many Americans aren't able to do so even if they want to.

As in many US cities, my neighborhood has been gentrified since the 1990s, meaning that many people who used to live here can no longer afford to and therefore now live someplace less convenient. And only blocks away from me, residents of more modest means do not have ready access to the amenities I just described above. The left and the right fight all the time over why this is. The left says gentrification is the enemy, while the right claims progressive politics are limiting upward mobility. Whoever is correct, the result is undeniable: much more than when I was a young journalist and urban planner first exploring these issues, cities have become the province of the rich and the poor.

As somebody who has always loved cities, I am saddened by the way cities today also separate the rich and the poor. I am saddened by the left-right debate as well. I do not believe, for example, that investment in a city neighborhood is inevitably bad for those who live there, though sometimes it is. Nor do I think that upward mobility in cities is limited these days because of the way those cities are governed, though sometimes it is.

The problems of gentrification and displacement in cities today are the result of the larger societal trend toward inequality, and it may be asking too much of a city to overcome those trends and correct all the problems. At the same time, cities are incredibly complex organisms—the result, simultaneously, of decades and centuries of construction on the one hand and, on the other, the day-to-day and even minute-by-minute decisions by millions of people living their lives. Given how complex cities are, the fact that they work at all—for anybody—is a miracle. The fact that they don't work for everybody these days is a tragedy.

In 1997, in the conclusion to *The Reluctant Metropolis*, I criticized what I called "cocoon citizenship"—essentially, the typical suburban habit of strip-mining cities for their amenities and then retreating to their residential cocoons to protect themselves once they are done consuming urban life. In a way, of course, that's what urban residents of means—like myself—do today: We live close to the amenities of urban life that we like, but use our cars and our walls and our locks and our security systems to block ourselves off from those aspects of urban life that we don't like and from people who are different from us. So even though we are urbanites, we don't engage fully in the life of the city. We are urban consumers but not urban citizens.

Cities today are in a different position than they were when I started writing about them in the 1980s. They're no longer at the bottom. Many of them are at the top—perhaps so high that they are beginning to topple over. Affluent residents in cities are clearly engaged in what sociologists have come to call "opportunity hoarding"—gathering urban amenities around them in a way that excludes others. And too many people are being left behind.

I don't know whether cities can solve all our society's problems. But I do know that they are resilient. They've been buffeted over the decades by White flight, decay, urban renewal, unequal investment, increasingly extreme weather events, and now the worst pandemic in a century, and they're still going strong. At their best, they not only inspire and uplift us, but they make our daily life more convenient and more fulfilling.

At a time when the rich-poor divide is troubling, maybe cities *can* go a long way toward taming inequality. But only if we give something back to them. Instead of just consuming them, each of us needs to invest in them—as citizens, as activists, and as people. Because cities, imposing though they may be as physical environments, don't work without *us*. For urbanism to succeed, we all have to participate in making cities great places for everybody.

Acknowledgments

The essays that appear in this book were written over a long period for many different reasons and appeared in many different publications and websites. The names of people who helped me conceive and write these essays is far too long to list here, but I would like to thank a few of them for their inspiration and support. Most are true urbanists, often laboring under arduous conditions to make our cities and towns better.

Rick Cole, who wrote the introduction, and Alan Ehrenhalt, who was for many years my editor at *Governing* magazine, have been friends and sources of inspiration for decades.

In Auburn, I am especially grateful to Mike Long, the former planning director and city manager, who helped guide me through Auburn's urban history and see Auburn from an urbanist's perspective as well as a native's perspective.

In Ventura, where I lived most of my adult life, I am grateful not only to Rick Cole, who served as city manager for my entire time on the city council, but also to Ventura's fine urban planners, especially Jeff Lambert, and my fellow council members Carl Morehouse, Sandy Smith, and especially Brian Brennan for their passion about both the urban and the natural environment in that gem of a small city.

In San Diego, I am thankful for a wonderful group of people who helped me understand both place and prosperity there, including Howard Blackson, Tom Tomlinson, Steve Russell, Liz Studebaker, David Graham, Mary Walshok, and especially Mayor Todd Gloria, who is leading the city into the next phase of its urbanism in an inspiring way.

In Houston, I want to thank the hearty band of urbanists trying to make the city more walkable and livable, including Christof Spieler, Amar Mohite, James Llamas, Geoff Carleton, my former student Marissa Aho, Jie Wu, and—until he left to run the Center for Transportation Studies at the University of Minnesota—my Kinder Institute colleague Kyle Shelton. All live urbanism in Houston more truly than I do, and all have inspired me.

Elsewhere in Texas, I want to thank Cullum Clark in Dallas, Steven Pedigo in Austin, and Henry Cisneros in San Antonio, my friend of more than thirty-five years, for their passion and insight into the ways place and prosperity intersect.

Along the way, I have had the privilege of being part of a remarkable group of urban planning academics who have sharpened my understanding of cities in a profound way. I am especially grateful to Marlon Boarnet and Dowell Myers at the University of Southern California; Rolf Pendall at the University of Illinois; Mai Nguyen at the University of California, San Diego; John Landis during his days at both the University of California, Berkeley and the University of Pennsylvania; Eugenie Birch, who is also at Penn; Brian Taylor and Evy Blumenberg at the University of California, Los Angeles; Gerrit Knapp at the University of Maryland; Bruce Appleyard at San Diego State University; and the late Robert E. Lang at the University of Nevada, Las Vegas. We all miss Rob very much.

I am also very grateful to my editor at Island Press, Heather Boyer. Many years ago, she put Peter Calthorpe and me together to write *The Regional City*, and I have always been grateful for that inspiration. She believed that I had another book in me even when I did not, and she tolerated many fits and starts in the preparation of this manuscript.

I am constantly inspired by both my daughter, Brooke Ezra Torf-Fulton, and my stepdaughter, Sophia Ramos-Paulin. Brooke loves *place* more than anyone I know and brings her sense of place (and her training in urban planning) to bear every day in her career as a healer. Although she is studying to be a biomedical engineer, Sophia is a big-city girl through and through, and I love seeing new cities and urban experiences through her eyes.

Finally, I am grateful most of all to my wife, Natalie. Our love of urban life is part of what brought us together in the first place. There is nothing more fun that exploring a new city with her, whether it is New York, Edinburgh, San Diego, or just some new neighborhood in Houston. I can't wait to see what experiences—and what cities—the future brings us.

Credits

Chapter 1, "The Making of an Urbanist," and Chapter 9, "My Favorite Street," were originally published on Medium.com (https://billfulton00 .medium.com).

Chapter 3, "The Garden Suburb and New Urbanism," was originally published in Parsons, Kermit C., and David Schuyler, eds. *From Garden City to Green City: The Legacy of Ebenezer Howard.* pp. 159–170. © 2002 Johns Hopkins University Press. Reprinted with permission of Johns Hopkins University Press.

Chapter 4, "The Autocratic Citizen of Philadelphia," Chapter 5, "Having No Car but Plenty of Cars," Chapter 6, "Tom Hayden's Cars," and an earlier version of Chapter 13, "Kotkin versus Florida," all originally appeared in *California Planning & Development Report* (www.cp-dr .com).

Chapter 6, "Talk City," originally appeared in *Talk City* (Solimar Books, 2017).

Chapter 8, "Why I'm Scared to Walk in Houston," originally appeared in *Urban Edge* (https://kinder.rice.edu/urban-edge).

Chapter 10, "Romancing the Smokestack," originally appeared in *Romancing the Smokestack* (Solimar Books, 2010).

Chapter 15, "The Long Drive," was originally published as part of *The Reluctant Metropolis: The Politics of Urban Growth in Los Angeles* (Solano Press Books, 1997; Johns Hopkins University Press, 2001).

Chapter 16, "The California Attitude," was originally published as part of *California: Land and Legacy* (Westcliffe Publishing, 1998).

Chapter 17, "The Not-So-Reluctant Metropolis," originally appeared in the paperback edition of *The Reluctant Metropolis: The Politics of Urban Growth in Los Angeles* (Johns Hopkins University Press, 2001).

Chapter 18, "Living the 2 Percent Life," originally appeared in Southern California Association of Governments' *State of the Region* report (2004).

Chapter 19, "My Los Angeles," originally appeared in *Planning* magazine (https://www.planning.org/planning/).

About the Author

William Fulton is one of America's most established thought leaders in the field of urban planning. From 2014 to 2022, he served as the director of Rice University's Kinder Institute for Urban Research. He is a former mayor of Ventura, California, and director of planning and economic development for the City of San Diego. His previous books include *Guide to California Planning*, the standard urban planning textbook in California; *The Reluctant Metropolis: The Politics of Urban Growth in Los Angeles*, which was a *Los Angeles Times* best seller; and *The Regional City: Planning for the End of Sprawl* (with Peter Calthorpe). Fulton holds master's degrees in mass communication from the American University and urban planning from UCLA.

Index